Praise for *Every Day Is an Audition*

Full of thoughtful insight and loving advice, *Every Day Is an Audition* is the book I wish someone had given me the day I left for college. It's the book I'll give my son the day he does.
—CHAD GIBBS, author of *God & Football* and *Love Thy Rival*

No matter your age or stage in life, *Every Day Is an Audition* is a must-read. This terrific book about life, love, faith, and family is a lot like its author—thoughtful and funny. In a world that badly needs it, this book is inspiring and empowering, entertaining and uplifting, and it will give all who read it encouragement for today and hope for tomorrow. Ric is a good friend, and this is a great book. I highly recommend it.
—JAY JACOBS, director of athletics, Auburn University

Every Day Is an Audition reads like a conversation with a wise and caring soul who has been there and struggled with many of life's big issues. Young people navigating college and their young adult lives will appreciate the humor and candor with which Ric Smith approaches serious topics. *Every Day Is an Audition* offers a friendly, Christian perspective on very worldly challenges.
—KIMBERLY SMOAK, campus director, South Carolina Teaching Fellows at USC

A poignant collection of short letters on life, love, and self-discovery. This book will tug at your heartstrings and challenge your thinking in a positive way.
—LESLIE HALLIN NESLAGE, marketing consultant, Chick-fil-A, Inc.

Practical perspective from a teacher and father. Ric Smith's advice should be required reading for every college student in America.
—STEPHEN NESLAGE, producer, "Wake up with Al" on The Weather Channel

EVERY DAY IS AN AUDITION

To Lisa—

Grace and Peace

Lee Smith

EVERY DAY IS
AN AUDITION

Thoughts on Life, Love, and Faith, for College and Beyond

RIC SMITH

Published by
Deep River Books
Sisters, Oregon
www.deepriverbooks.com

ISBN - 13: 9781940269061
ISBN - 10: 1940269067

Library of Congress: 2013954575

Printed in the USA

Cover design by David Litwin, Purefusion Media

ACKNOWLEDGMENTS

I could not and did not write this book alone. I am grateful to family and friends who have encouraged me and supported me in ways I could never have imagined. I am humbled and honored to have you in my life. With apologies to George Bailey, I am the richest man in town.

Thank you to Barbara and James Barnett; Dink and Preston Barnett; Lynn and Matthew Bradakis; Mary Helen Brown and Beth Yarbrough; Ellen and Eric Canada; Lucinda Cannon; Rhonda and Kevin Dougherty; Susan Fillippeli; Anita Floyd; Jean and Bruce Heath; Jane and Steve Henley; Kathryn and Larry Hipp; Laurie and Jim Keffer; Sara Nan and Jim Levins; Diane and Tom McMahon; Leslie and Stephen Neslage; Frances and Tommy Palmer; Dorothy and William Perryman; Sandra and Wayne Smith; Kim Smoak; and Laura and Kyle Travis.

As everyone who knows me will agree, I married above myself. Thank you to my lovely wife, Carole. And thank you to my wonderful son, Harry. I love you and am very proud of you (pfffffft).

—Ric Smith

To Harry

CONTENTS

LOVE

FAITH

INTRODUCTION

But I tell you the truth that everyone will have to give an account
on the day of judgment for every empty word they have spoken.
For by your words you will be acquitted,
and by your words you will be condemned.
MATTHEW 12:36-37

It is the writer's privilege to help man endure by lifting his heart.
WILLIAM FAULKNER

This book began as a collection of letters for my wonderful son, Harry. I wrote the letters over a period of a few months (a couple of years actually), had the collection bound, and gave it to him for his birthday. I wanted to share with him some of the things I've come to know in life. I've done a few things right and a quite a few things wrong, so this book was a way for him to learn from my experiences. It wasn't intended to be a lifestyle manual or a set of directions, I just wanted to give Harry a few things to think about, and I wanted to create an opportunity for the two of us to talk about life and love and faith.

The idea to publish the letters came from my students at Auburn University where I teach in the School of Communication and Journalism. I have what I call "Tea Time" with my students. It's a time to get together after class to talk about whatever is on their minds. Also, my lovely wife, Carole, and I will invite students over for supper on a regular basis. During these "Tea Times" and talks around the table,

13

the discussion will often turn to career, marriage, and God. I've shared Harry's letters with students (Harry said it was okay) and they've often said they would like to have a collection for themselves. So here it is.

I've maintained the original tone as much as possible because I think it makes each letter more conversational. And that's how I see this book—a collection of seeds for conversation. I've tried to be honest and, at times, even blunt. Young adults (like you) expect, and deserve, adult-level conversation. It's my assumption you're setting out on your new adult life and you're going through the process of sorting out all of the issues that come with being on your own. To speak with you at anything less than an adult level would be disrespectful. I'm sure you get enough of that as it is. Welcome to grown up world. Fasten your seat belt and keep your hands inside the vehicle throughout the ride.

Please keep in mind *Every Day Is an Audition* is not intended to be read as a novel. I think it works best to read the letters one or two at a time, then spend time praying, pondering, thinking, considering, and perhaps discussing in a small group setting. You will probably read statements in this book you don't agree with. That's okay. In fact, since quite a few of the letters deal with some combination of God, sex, and politics, that is inevitable. Differences of opinion present a wonderful opportunity for conversation and community. Christians don't always agree (How's that for stating the obvious?), but we must always love each other as Christ loves us. Sometimes that love will be seasoned with salt; yet it must always be filled with grace.

The writing of these letters required a tremendous amount of spiritual, emotional, and physical energy. I take every statement in this book seriously, and I am secure in what I have written. Having said that, let me say I humbly acknowledge I have much to learn. Each day God presents opportunities for me to grow and mature. I pray always for ears to hear and eyes to see.

Grace and Peace,

Ric Smith

LIFE

GRADES DON'T MATTER
(WELL . . . SORT OF)

For wisdom will enter your heart, and knowledge
will be pleasant to your soul.
PROVERBS 2:10

Education is what survives when what has been
learnt has been forgotten.
B.F. SKINNER

G rades don't matter. And now that I have your attention . . . what I really mean is that grades are not the most important thing. Learning is much more important. Oddly enough, learning and good grades don't always go together.

There will be some people in school who absolutely obsess over studying. They'll spend what seems like every waking minute in the library. And I don't mean that as a knock against libraries. In fact, I love them. I love the thought of all that knowledge and wisdom right at my fingertips. I even love that musty old book smell. Libraries are wonderful places filled with great resources.

However, I see two problems with spending your entire college career in the library. The first problem is those hard-studying people may be so focused on making a grade, they don't really learn the material beyond what is required to regurgitate it back onto the test. That's not really learning, it's just short-term memorization. Don't study merely because you're trying to achieve a certain letter or number on an assignment. You don't have to earn a 4.0 grade point average. The closest I got to a 4.0 in college was my blood alcohol content (that's a joke). Study because you care about the subject. Good grades will come from that and so will good learning.

The second problem is good grades don't always translate into practical application. For many majors, you'll also need experience and you can't get experience in the library. Get involved with campus and professional activities that give you the opportunity to get your hands dirty . . . to actually do what you're learning to do. Those activities may take away from study time, but that's okay because practical experience is a valuable part of your education, too.

An old college buddy of mine used to say, "Never let your education get in the way of college." That's just a funny way of saying you should get everything out of college it has to offer . . . both in class and out. What happens in the classroom is very important, but I think it's safe to say at least half of college is what happens outside of class.

When you make it to graduation (which will come much sooner than you can imagine), you'll be stunned at how much you've changed. In fact, you'll grow more in your four years of college than you did in the eighteen years it took you to get there. And that's what education is all about . . . learning and changing . . . growing mentally . . . socially . . . and spiritually.

Now let me make something perfectly clear: In no way am I saying it's okay to make bad grades. Go to the library (again, it's a wonderful place). Study. Work hard. Focus on the most important things . . . perhaps even focus on your GPA to some degree. While it is true practical experience is important, it is also true your grade point average is not unimportant. Many internships have minimum requirements. Graduate and professional schools will definitely have minimum requirements. You may be asked about your GPA when applying for jobs. Your grades may be used by some as a barometer of your ability. That number could be the difference between you or a competing applicant getting the position.

The point is this: You can get good experience and still make good grades. Those things are not mutually exclusive. And a bad GPA is a strong indication that something is wrong . . . like you're not working hard enough or you're in the wrong major.

✓ You'll grow more in your four years of college than you did in the eighteen years it took to get there. And that's what education is all about . . . learning and changing . . . growing mentally . . . socially . . . and spiritually.

But in the end, it's not the number that matters, it's the quality of your education. Take courses that challenge you. It's much better to make a B in a course you'll benefit from than an A in a GPA boosting class like Underwater Basket Weaving. Try new things (within reason). Meet new people. Get involved. Travel. Make the most of this marvelous opportunity.

One more thing: There will be some required classes you may not enjoy and there will be some classes you would rather not take. That's just part of receiving a well-rounded education (and sometimes you'll be surprised how much you enjoy a class you never would have taken had it not been required). There will be times you will be frustrated, overwhelmed, exhausted, and won't feel like studying. Do it anyway.

Here's a checklist that may help you make your way through college. This list does not include everything, but it does include some important things you don't want to miss.

Go to class . . . every day.

Read the textbook before class then review the notes after class.

Read the syllabus.

Get to know your professors (some will be more open and available than others).

Plan ahead . . . and never fall behind.

Eat well, exercise, and get plenty of rest. It is very difficult to do . . . especially during mid-terms and finals.

Get involved in campus activities and professional activities . . . the more experience you gain the better.

Meet new people . . . go new places . . . try new things . . . *at least* half of your education is what happens outside of the classroom.

Find a faith community.

Follow your passion . . . you just have to figure out how to make a living at it.

You are about to go on the ride of your life . . . have fun . . . remember who you are . . . discover who you will become.

Things to Think About:

✓ What's the difference between memorization and knowledge?

✓ What practical experience could you gain to complement your course work?

✓ How do you balance school time, work time, and personal time?

✓ Do you study with other people? How can you best learn with and from others? How can others best learn with and from you? What's the downside to studying in groups?

WHAT YOU KNOW

If anyone builds on this foundation using gold, silver, costly
stones, wood, hay or straw, their work will be shown for what it is,
because the Day will bring it to light. It will be revealed with fire,
and the fire will test the quality of each person's work.
I CORINTHIANS 3:12-13

An education isn't how much you have committed to memory, or
even how much you know. It's being able to differentiate between
what you know and what you don't.
ANATOLE FRANCE

There's an old saying related to finding a job that goes, "It's not what you know, it's who you know." The idea is that you find a job based on connections, not ability. Well, that's only half right. Who you know matters, of course. Contacts are important. But what you know is essential.

As you move into the working world, you will find people who were hired because they knew the right person. Or, more likely, their parents knew the right person. There is some uncle, or politician, or family connection who gives "Junior" a job as a favor to the family. The result is usually pretty darn ugly. The problem is that if Junior is hired solely on the basis of his family's influence, he won't make it. He won't have the skills and talent for the job (and probably won't have the right attitude either). So he will flounder around for a while and ultimately fail.

And that's why the "what you know" is so important. You've got to know what you're doing so you can actually do what you've been hired to do. I know that sounds rather obvious, but I've seen it happen.

Develop your skills and hone your talents. Work hard and work smart. Start small, move up, and make a name for yourself by demonstrating a maturity beyond your years, a sense of urgency in your work, and an ability to solve problems along the way.

You'll succeed because you'll be good at what you do. And the better you are at what you do, the more likely it is that someone will recommend you for the job. Your reputation will precede you. And that's going to work for (or against) ol' Junior too. His reputation will precede him.

✓ Develop your skills and hone your talents. Work hard and work smart. Start small, move up, and make a name for yourself by demonstrating a maturity beyond your years, a sense of urgency in your work, and an ability to solve problems along the way.

There's also a personal benefit to gaining experience. As you begin to work in your field, you'll find out if you really like it and are any good at it. You'll find your ability and passion . . . or not. And it's better to figure that out now rather than a few years down the line. Some professions look very different from the outside than they do from the inside. Your dream job may look all cool, glamorous, and glitzy when you're sitting on the couch, but it's shockingly different when you're doing it every day. It's sort of like swimming. You can study swimming all you want . . . buoyancy, strokes, competition . . . but the reality is you don't truly understand swimming until your butt is in the deep end of the pool.

One last thought on this idea: Sometimes the "Juniors" of the world hang on. And, oddly enough, sometimes they even move up. I've known some absolute morons who have somehow made it into influential positions and manage to stay there (and maybe they think the same thing about me). But you have to worry about yourself and what is right for you. You can't concern yourself with ol' Junior. It's like an old friend of mine used to say . . . you just have to overlook folks like that.

Things to Think About:

✓ How do you go about gaining practical experience?

✓ What practical experience do you have? How has it been helpful? If very little practical experience, why?

✓ What are employers looking for when making a hire? Why are they interested in maturity, urgency, and problem solving skills?

✓ What makes you the right person for the job? Why should they hire you?

✓ Have you ever known one of those "Juniors" of the world? How did it go?

WHO YOU KNOW

As iron sharpens iron, so one person sharpens another.
PROVERBS 27:17

The currency of real networking is not greed but generosity.
KEITH FERRAZZI

This is the other side of the "what you know" conversation. As I've said, who you know does matter. It's good to get to know people in your field . . . that's called networking.

Networking begins as you build relationships . . . in major classes . . . in campus activities . . . in professional groups . . . in jobs. It's amazing what a small world it is and how frequently the same people keep coming around. In virtually every profession you'll get the feeling that everybody knows everybody. And without question, everybody does know everybody within two or three degrees of separation.

As you meet people along the way, get to know them. Make an effort to develop relationships. Hold on to telephone numbers and email addresses. Get involved with professional development organizations and associations. You'll be surprised how many opportunities will come along because of who you know . . . and who knows you.

The way I've described this idea so far makes it sound like you meet people so they can help you. Well, that's true to a degree, but it's certainly not everything. Be a resource to them as well. You should always think of networking as building mutually-beneficial two-way relationships. Each person is willing to help the other. There are people I went to college with who I still touch base with from time to time. They continue to help me and I continue to help them. So networking begins now and continues throughout your life.

There's one other aspect to this networking idea. You're at a place in life where you probably need more help than you're able to return. After all, you are just now getting started in your adult life. At this point, you are more likely to be helped by someone who has much more experience and influence than you, so it would be virtually impossible for you to pay them back (although you just never know what may happen down the line). But having said that, I think there are two ways you can pay them back even now.

As you meet people along the way, get to know them. Make an effort to develop relationships. Hold on to telephone numbers and email addresses. Get involved with professional development organizations and associations. You'll be surprised how many opportunities will come along because of who you know . . . and who knows you.

First, always say thank you. Write a note (a real letter, not email). I promise they will notice . . . if you do and if you don't. Maybe take them to lunch. Just do something to let them know you appreciate what they have done for you.

The second thing you can do is pay it forward. Pay back the person who helped you by helping the next generation that is coming along. You'll mean as much to the person you help as your mentor means to you. And that starts now. Be willing to help out younger people who are trying to figure things out. For example, it only takes one year of college or one year on the job for you to be in a position to help the new class of first year students or the new hires who join you at work (and they'll be just as overwhelmed as you were and just as determined to cover it up . . . don't ever forget that feeling). It never ends. There is always someone younger and less experienced who could benefit from your knowledge and wisdom. All you have to do is make yourself mindful and available.

Things to Think About:

✓ How do you go about building professional relationships?

✓ How do you organize and manage your contacts?

✓ What is one example of a professional relationship you have developed?

✓ How can you "pay it forward" now? Is there someone you have mentored?

DARE TO BE DIFFERENT

When the angel of the LORD appeared to Gideon, he said,
'The LORD is with you, mighty warrior.'
JUDGES 6:12

To be nobody but yourself in a world which is doing its best, night
and day, to make you everybody else, means to fight the hardest
battle which any human being can fight; and never stop fighting.
E. E. CUMMINGS

Everyone wants to fit in. We like being part of a group and we want to belong. It's important to have friends . . . and to be a friend. That's just part of being human. People are social creatures, so get out and join up. Be involved. Find your place.

When I was a freshman in college, I really didn't do that. I had some terrific friends and I had a wonderful time at school. I learned a lot, but I wasn't very active in campus life. When I graduated and moved on to school at Auburn University, I got involved with the student radio station, WEGL, and it was terrific. In many ways it was life changing. I met great people, I learned more than I ever thought I would, and I had fun doing it, too. After a couple of years at WEGL, I was selected as station manager, so I was able to make a contribution as a campus leader. I didn't just participate, I contributed. And, without a doubt, it's the single best thing I did in college.

That's where I found my fit, and you'll find yours in the place that is unique to you. It really depends on your personality and where you feel most comfortable. You'll just have to figure out what that is. How would you describe your personality? What's important to you? Where do you feel most comfortable?

So what happens if you're thinking about joining up, or maybe you're already in, and you realize you just don't feel right there? That's okay. Finding groups to belong to and the friends who usually come along with them is like dating in a way (and that's likely to be where some of your dates come from). You'll try out quite a few before the right one comes along. Just like people, groups have distinct personalities. There are social groups, business groups, hobby groups, religious groups, political groups, volunteer groups, sports groups, support groups, youth groups, and senior groups of all shapes and sizes. Sometimes you'll know from the outside a particular place is not the one for you. Other times, you'll have to see it from the inside. There are situations, too, where the group was right at the time you joined, but you and/or they changed along the way, so there came a time to move on.

One other thing to keep in mind is that while it's true you have the option to join (or not) many groups, there will be some you're just thrown into. Your family is a group you didn't choose (although I'm sure they are very glad to have you as a member). You didn't choose your hometown (your parents chose that for you). Even in college, you'll be assigned to certain groups based on where you live and your chosen major. That will also be true in your professional life. Oftentimes in life, there are natural connections of people that come with the circumstances of life. It's not so much we intentionally join, it's more that we find ourselves together in school, in work, in community. Do your best to contribute your unique personality and talents however you can.

And that brings me (and not a moment too soon) to the point: As wonderful as groups can be, there can also be a danger that develops. A pack mentality may grow . . . on both sides. Sometimes we want to fit in because it's easier that way . . . easier to go along to get along.

31

It's safe. It's comfortable. We blend in and may even become invisible, losing our unique identity. On the other hand, once we're in, we may feel we're trapped and can't get out. It may be they don't want to let go when the time to move on does come around. People from groups can become very possessive—even controlling—and that's a problem.

✓ If you step out to find your own way, if you are determined to do what is best, if you distinguish yourself, you'll find there are people who will throw stones at you. Get ready. It's coming.

If you find that happening, it would be nice to think the group likes you and doesn't want to lose you, and that may very well be the case. And it's easy to understand, of course, why a group would want to hold on to an important member. No team wants to lose a star player. But even when a player leaves, it's always much better to celebrate the time everyone had together and to wish each other well as all move on to new things than it is to be spiteful and hold grudges.

The reality is, however, it's not always quite so nice. Often you'll find they would rather hold you back than move forward themselves . . . it's easier for them that way. Let's face it, change is hard. As you begin to grow they begin to see themselves in a different light. They are challenged . . . and a lot of people in this world don't like to be challenged. So if you step out to find your own way, if you are determined to do what is best, if you distinguish yourself, you'll find there are people who will throw stones at you. Get ready. It's coming.

Ralph Waldo Emerson wrote in his essay *Self Reliance*,[1] "Is it so bad then to be misunderstood? Pythagoras was misunderstood, and Socrates, and Jesus, and Luther, and Copernicus, and Galileo, and

Newton, and every pure and wise spirit that ever took flesh. To be great is to be misunderstood." The great people of the world have always been unique. Not merely for the sake of being different (that's its own problem), but because they were willing to be true to themselves, to not fall in with the crowd. If you're an exceptional person, you're going to stand out. You have to—that's what makes you an exception. Dare to be different.

One more thing: Don't ever let anyone tell you that you can't do something you aspire to do or that you'll never make it. That attitude says much more about them than it does about you.

Things to Think About:

✓ What groups have you belonged to that made you a better person? How did you find them or how did they find you?

✓ Have you ever felt held back or limited by a group?

✓ Why did you leave the groups you are no longer a part of? What was the reaction of the group?

✓ Have you ever been mad because someone left your group? How did it end? How can you be encouraging to someone who is moving on?

EVERY DAY IS AN AUDITION

Likewise, every good tree bears good fruit, but a bad tree bears
bad fruit. A good tree cannot bear bad fruit, and a
bad tree cannot bear good fruit. Every tree that does not bear
good fruit is cut down and thrown into the fire.
Thus, by their fruit you will recognize them.
MATTHEW 7:17-20

The future is not some place we are going, but one we create.
The paths are not found, but made, and the activity of making
them changes both the maker and the destination.
JOHN SCHAAR

One of the happiest days of my life was when I was asked to be the stadium announcer for Auburn University football. And just for the record, marrying my lovely wife, Carole, and my wonderful son, Harry, being born are the top two. Just behind that is the day I was asked to announce the Southeastern Conference Football Championship. For anyone who has ever done any type of announcing (and even people who just dream of announcing), those are two of the best jobs in the country. I am very fortunate to be where I am. The funny thing is, I didn't really apply for either of those jobs.

I first got involved with radio when I was a student at Auburn working with the campus station, WEGL (remember to get experience). From there I had a variety of announcing related gigs through the years. I was asked to announce Opelika High School football games.

That sounded like fun (and it was), so I did that for a few years. During that time I was taking a graduate class and I had a classmate named Jeremy Roberts. Jeremy worked in marketing for the athletics department and was responsible for baseball. One evening in class I made a presentation, so Jeremy heard me use my big-boy announcer voice. (People often comment that my regular voice is so much different from my stadium voice, but I think it would be rather strange if I talked that way all the time . . . HELLO, IT'S SO GOOD TO SEE YOU . . . it would be weird to always speak in capital letters). That presentation led to a conversation where he asked about the work I do and asked if I would be interested in announcing Auburn University baseball games. That sounded like fun (and it was), so I did that for a few years.

 Every day is an audition. You never know who is watching. You never know who is listening. Give it all you've got . . . every day.

In the spring of 2006 Jeremy called and said he wanted to talk with me about something and asked if we could meet the next day (he had taken on football responsibilities by this time). When we met, he said legendary Jordan-Hare Stadium announcer Carl Stephens[2] was retiring and asked if I would be interested in taking his place at the microphone. Of course I said yes . . . although I'm not exactly sure what that "yes" sounded like because it's hard to talk when your heart is about to leap out of your chest.

Jeremy had heard my work during the five years I announced Auburn baseball, so he knew what I could do. I didn't audition the day of our meeting. I auditioned one game at a time for five years. My first game was September 2, 2006: Auburn v. Washington State.

About halfway through the 2006 season I got a telephone call from Craig Mattox of the Southeastern Conference. They were looking for someone to announce the SEC football championship. Craig happened to be at an Auburn football game that Saturday (I had never met Craig and had no idea he was there . . . or even who he was for that matter), so he heard me announce the game (those speakers are so darn powerful, I'm rather hard to miss). He said my style matched what the SEC was looking for and asked if I was interested in announcing the championship game in Atlanta. Yes, please.

This story is a long way of telling you every day is an audition. You never know who is watching. You never know who is listening. Give it all you've got . . . every day.

Things to Think About:

✓ Have you ever considered that people are always watching?

✓ How difficult is it to "give it all you've got" everyday?

✓ Have you ever been offered an opportunity that you didn't see coming? How did it happen?

WHAT DO YOU WANT TO BE WHEN YOU GROW UP?

Then Jesus said to his disciples: 'Therefore I tell you,
do not worry about your life, what you will eat; or about your body,
what you will wear. For life is more than food,
and the body more than clothes.'
LUKE 12:22-23

Don't be one of those timid souls who says, 'If only I had my life
to live over.' Live your life in such a way that once is enough.
WALTER CUNNINGHAM

What do you want to be when you grow up? That was a question you heard a lot as a kid. In college the question is, what do you want to major in? It's the same question asked in a different way. The real question they are asking is, what are you going to do for a living? What are you going to do for money? In our culture we often define ourselves, or are defined by others, by our professions. If you ask people to describe themselves they will usually begin by talking about their jobs. "I work at the bank." "I'm a lawyer." "I teach." And it's rather odd if you think about it because most people would stop working if they had the chance. If they were presented a great inheritance or won the lottery, they would immediately quit their jobs. In fact, I know people who hate their jobs. They go to work Monday morning wishing it was Friday afternoon. They live for the weekend. And if you do the math, that doesn't make much sense. They are wishing away five-sevenths of their lives. Life is too short as it is. So it seems to me that if someone is living for the weekend, they are in the wrong profession. Their jobs are not "them" at all.

It is necessary to work for a living, of course. Most of us are not independently wealthy after all. We need money for a home and car. We need money to take care of our families and to buy food and clothes. And there are some luxuries we would like to enjoy. You know, vacations, electronic toys, and that sort of thing. It's good to be financially responsible and self-sufficient as we go about the business of living. But keep in mind that although money helps us do those things we want or buy what we need, the desire for money should never be our only purpose for working.

Also remember you should never choose a profession hoping for admiration or social standing. True respect comes from who you are, not what you do. And if you ever meet someone (and you will) who likes you only if you live in the "right neighborhood," drive the "right car," or have the "right job," don't worry about them. They'll be too shallow to worry about.

Here's my suggestion. Assume for a moment you are independently wealthy. I don't mean filthy rich . . . just that you have enough money to live at a level that makes you reasonably comfortable. You can afford the necessities and maybe a couple of luxuries (and by luxuries I don't mean caviar, private jets, and vacations in Bermuda; I'm talking about an occasional steak on the grill, a dependable car, and a few days at the beach). If you had that, what would you do? How would you spend your time? If you were free to be yourself, what would you be . . . who would you be? Whatever your answer is, find a way to match that up with your career. If you do that you will be true to yourself. You will answer your calling. You will find a way to "make a living" by being yourself.

That's the difference between working to live (meeting obligations) and living to work (accomplishing what is important to you). Keep in mind, you probably won't be the wealthiest person in town. You may have to make some financial sacrifices. But it seems to me that being true to yourself and following your calling is no sacrifice at all.

You should never choose a profession hoping for admiration or social standing. True respect comes from who you are, not what you do.

One more thing: One of the first things that happens when you get to college is you're asked to declare a major. I understand why that's necessary since you must get started on the path to graduation, but the problem is you're just starting out so you don't really know anything yet. That's not an insult, it's just that you haven't had the chance to be out on your own to grow and learn. How can you decide what you want to major in . . . what you want to do for the rest of your life . . . when you don't even know who you are yet?

While it's true some people do know right from the start (and that's great for them), most do not. Don't be afraid to put off that decision until you've had a chance to try a few classes. There are certain foundational classes everyone takes and those will give you some good ideas. You'll also have a few electives you can use. And once you have declared a major, you may find you're in the wrong place and need to make a change. I actually changed direction in graduate school, moving from political science to communication.

Having said all of that . . . you can't stay in college forever. There will come a time when you'll be kicked out into the real world. And once you do join the real world and begin your professional life, remember that what you do first you don't have to do forever. Just as it's okay to change majors, it's also okay to change jobs or even careers. I did that, too.

Things to Think About:

✓ What would you do if you suddenly became financially independent?

✓ What do you consider a "reasonable" style of living?

✓ Do you think there's a point where the money makes a bad job worth it? How much money? How bad of a job?

MONEY IS LIKE A SHOVEL

But godliness with contentment is great gain. For we brought
nothing into the world and we can take nothing out of it.
But if we have food and clothing we will be content with that.
Those who want to get rich fall into temptation and a trap and
into many foolish and harmful desires that plunge people into ruin
and destruction. For the love of money is the root of all kinds of
evil. Some people, eager for money, have wandered from the faith
and pierced themselves with many griefs. But you, man of God,
flee from all this, and pursue righteousness, godliness,
faith, love, endurance and gentleness.

I TIMOTHY 6:6-11.

The problem with being in the rat race is that
even if you win you're still a rat.

LILY TOMLIN

Money is a funny thing. Some people will do most anything to
get it . . . even cheat and steal. But I don't want to focus on
those who cheat and steal, I want to focus on people who are
not crooks at all. I'm talking about good people who would
never cheat and steal from others yet may be cheating and stealing from
themselves . . . people who sell out and sacrifice their lives for money
and who spend their lives grasping for money. It may sound odd to use
the phrase "spending their lives for money," but that's just what it is.
They spend their lives trying to get money to use . . . or hold on to.

I am very fortunate in that I like my job. I like what I do, I like where I do it, and I like who I do it with. I guess I could take another job and make more money. Or I could move to another town that offers other opportunities . . . but at what cost?

✔ Let me be clear about something: I don't mean to imply that having money is a bad thing. It's not. There is nothing inherently wrong in being wealthy. Money is neither good nor bad. It's what you do to get it and what you do when you have it that matters.

When I get home at the end of the day, I'm usually feeling pretty good because most days at work are good. I'm not physically and emotionally exhausted. That means I still have fuel in my tank for my family. I'm more than just some lump on the couch vegging out until bedtime. I don't travel much and I don't have many late night meetings. When my wonderful son, Harry, was a kid, it meant we could do things together . . . Boy Scouts, soccer games, and school plays.

Other things are important for us, too. Both sets of parents are close by, so we have always been able to spend time with them. Plus, we have friends we've known for many years. I can't put a price tag on these relationships.

Of course, those choices come with their own costs. We have to understand we can't buy every sparkly delight we see. Sometimes we just can't afford certain things. And by the way, don't get the impression we are poor. We're not. Not even close. But it is true we can't buy whatever we want whenever we want it. We live within our means. We don't live in the biggest house or drive the fanciest car. We don't stay in the swankiest hotels or eat at five star restaurants (I'm just looking for a barbecue joint that passes the health inspection . . . and it doesn't have to be a high grade). We have a television but no home theater system. And that's okay. There is no question money will typically be a factor when making decisions, but it should never be the most important factor and certainly not the only factor.

Let me be clear about something: I don't mean to imply that having money is a bad thing. It's not. There is nothing inherently wrong in being wealthy. Money is neither good nor bad. It's what you do to get it and what you do when you have it that matters.

And understand, too, I'm talking about our family, not others. I can't speak for other people because I don't know what is right for them. You and your family will have to make those decisions for yourselves. You know what is right for you. My lovely wife, Carole, and I know what is right for us.

Now without a doubt we need money to live. We have financial obligations. We must eat and buy clothes. We want a comfortable place to live and a dependable car to drive. We have medical bills and expenses for education. And some fun stuff is okay, too. It's a matter of perspective, balance, and understanding that money is not the meaning of life.

Money is of no value in and of itself. So why hoard it? Why "spend your life" trying to get more than you could ever need? Would you ever hoard rakes, shovels, hammers, and saws? They are also tools.

Use the tool—money—to accomplish what is important in your life. But don't spend your life collecting shovels. All they will be good for is digging your grave.

Things to Think About:

✓ What is most valuable to you? Is it worth spending your life for?

✓ We often think about the cost of living (things we buy, bills we pay, etc.), but what are the opportunity costs connected to life's decisions?

✓ What is a reasonable standard of living for you?

TIME

For what it's worth: it's never too late or, in my case, too early
to be whoever you want to be. There's no time limit, stop
whenever you want. You can change or stay the same, there are
no rules to this thing. We can make the best or the worst of it.
I hope you make the best of it. And I hope you see things
that startle you. I hope you feel things you never felt before.
I hope you meet people with a different point of view. I hope
you live a life you're proud of. If you find that you're not,
I hope you have the courage to start all over again.
'BENJAMIN BUTTON' FROM THE MOVIE *THE CURIOUS CASE OF BENJAMIN BUTTON*

Time is the most valuable thing you possess. Of course, time is not a "thing" in the usual sense. You don't really own it or hold on to it. It's not a commodity like gold is a commodity, although it's actually more valuable than gold. You can count your gold, but you can't count your time. We have a particular amount of time on earth (however much that may be) and when it's up, it's up.

Related to that, I think it's interesting we think about age relative to when someone was born. We see a twenty-year-old as younger than a fifty-year-old. Yes, I know the twenty-year-old is chronologically younger, but there is another way of looking at it. What if the twenty-year-old had only ten years left to live, but the fifty-year-old had fifty more? In a sense, that makes the fifty-year-old younger. Since we don't know how much time we have, that makes every day invaluable . . . no matter how old or young you are.[3]

Time is unique in that if you lose it you can never get it back. Money is different. If you lose your money, you can earn more. If someone breaks into your house and takes your stuff, you can get more of what you had. If you wreck your car, you can have it repaired or go to the car lot and buy another one. You get the idea. But for time, once it's gone, it's gone forever.

What does this mean? Don't squander time. Honor the time you have—the gift of life God has given you—by using it wisely. Okay, what does that mean? Well, to me it means spending time on things that are important or things I enjoy. And I must admit sometimes the things that are important may not be all that enjoyable, but there is a satisfaction that comes from doing them. For example, our wonderful son, Harry, is an extremely important part of our life and his mom and I would do anything for him—it's important. When he was a baby he had problems with ear infections, so we spent a lot of nights staying up with him. It was not enjoyable. In fact, it was downright miserable. But it was important because we love Harry and he needed us. Plus, I find great satisfaction in knowing I was able to take care of him.

Work is an important part of this idea, too, because it requires so much of our time. It seems to me, if you're working forty hours a week (and it will likely be more), you should feel good about what you're doing. Not just punching the clock, but building something or making a contribution in some way. Work should be more than merely putting in the hours and picking up a paycheck.

Unfortunately, for many people that is not the case and I think there are a number of reasons why that happens. For some it's a matter of options (actually, a lack of options . . . that's one reason your education is so important . . . education provides options and opportunities).

And let me say here I do understand some people just don't have a choice. I realize some people are lucky to have the jobs they do have and I realize some people don't have jobs at all . . . and it's not for a lack of trying. There are some people who are giving it everything they've got and are barely scraping by. I have great admiration for the sacrifices they make to provide for their families . . . but that's not really who I'm talking about.

✓ My work is important and fulfilling. That's a wonderful combination. I find that I feel good at the end of the day and I look forward to tomorrow. I still enjoy the weekend, but I enjoy the other five days, too. That is what I hope for you . . . whatever your calling and career may be.

I'm talking about people who are stuck because they choose to be stuck. It could be they have run up so much debt, they have no way of making a change. They've become slaves to their possessions . . . buying much more (McMansions, cars, boats, vacations) than they could reasonably afford and now are living paycheck to paycheck because of past decisions. They chose to go into debt and now they're living without options.

It could also be that inertia has set in. You know, a body at rest will stay at rest until acted on by an outside force. For some, it's easier to be miserable than make a change. I've been there. I know because I'm writing from experience.

There was a time when I was miserable in my work and when I spent the week wishing for the weekend. I made a career change that meant less money but more contentment. This career change meant less money but more freedom. It meant less money but a richer life. Fortunately, I am married to the most wonderful woman in the world who rode the wave as I made the change (it was actually more whiplash than change). And the cool thing is I was able to do the same for her a few years later.

This is not to say I never have bad days and it's not to say I don't get frustrated or aggravated sometimes. However, the key is to focus on the big picture and to keep everything in perspective. My work is important and fulfilling. That's a wonderful combination. I find that I feel good at the end of the day and I look forward to tomorrow. I still enjoy the weekend, but I enjoy the other five days, too. That is what I hope for you . . . whatever your calling and career may be.

Also keep in mind there is much more to life than good work and meaningful obligations, no matter how fulfilling they may be. Be sure you do some things just for the fun of it. Fun is good.

What I'm trying to say is life's too short to wish it away or let it slip away from you. Love your family. Do good work. Hang out with your friends. Go play. Enjoy life.

Things to Think About:

✓ What brings you the greatest satisfaction in life? What makes you miserable?

✓ Do you know someone (especially an older person) who has a positive attitude and seems to get the most out of life? What is it about the person that makes them different?

✓ What could you do (or continue doing) so that you have a positive attitude and get the most out of life?

✓ Take the Time Test on the following page to see if your perception of time matches the reality.

TIME TEST

Time is the only "possession" we have that when it is gone, it is gone. It can never be re-earned or replaced. This means time is our greatest gift to others because we are giving something of ourselves that is irreplaceable. The way we spend our time shows what is truly important to us. We may claim someone or something is important, but if we devote little or no time to that person or that purpose, how truly important could it be?

The left side column contains a variety of items most of us would consider important to some degree (feel free to add more). In the middle column, list the items in their order of importance to you. Over the next few weeks, keep a record of where you spend your time then rank the items accordingly in the far right column.

Bible/Faith Study _____ _____
Community Involvement _____ _____
Church Involvement _____ _____
Education/Personal Study _____ _____
Exercise _____ _____
Family (children) _____ _____
Family (spouse) _____ _____
Family (others) _____ _____
Friends _____ _____
Hobbies _____ _____
Internet _____ _____
Maintenance/Chores _____ _____
Prayer & Worship _____ _____
Reading _____ _____
Shopping _____ _____
Social Media _____ _____
TV & Video _____ _____
Work/Career _____ _____

THE MERELY GOOD

And this is my prayer: that your love may abound more and more
in knowledge and depth of insight, so that you may be able to
discern what is best and may be pure and blameless until the day
of Christ, filled with the fruit of righteousness that comes through
Jesus Christ—to the glory and praise of God.
PHILIPPIANS 1:9-11

The great enemy of the life of faith in God is not sin, but the good
which is not good enough. The good is always the enemy of the best.
OSWALD CHAMBERS

There will come a time in your life, and you're probably there already, where you'll find you have more to do than you can get done. There is work, family, friends, church, responsibilities, obligations, hobbies, and just general fun. And all of these things may be good in their own way. For example, at our house we have to clean, cut grass, pay bills, and all those other responsibilities and obligations that go into keeping up a home. I may not really want to cut the grass (especially in August), but I know it's part of being a homeowner and that is important to us. Taking care of our home is time-consuming, difficult, and expensive, but it's worth the investment. We do what we need to do knowing the relatively small sacrifice is for a greater good.

You know the old saying, "A job worth doing is worth doing well." If you're going to do something, you should put in the time and effort to do it to the best of your ability. But there is a problem here. It's possible to get to the point where you're doing so many things you can't do any of them well. It's like you're stomping out one fire after another, just hoping the whole thing doesn't blaze out of control. What should be good becomes stressful. It becomes just one more thing that has to be done. You'll find yourself dreading one more thing . . . then one more thing . . . then one more thing. That's when your head explodes.

Here's another problem you'll have to figure out if you're a person who is smart, responsible, and gracious (since you're reading this book, you are clearly those things and more) . . . smart, responsible, and gracious is a dangerous combination. What I mean is that since you are good at what you do, you do what you say you're going to do, and you're pleasant to work with, you're going to be given so many "opportunities" you'll have to be careful you don't drown. Because you are smart, responsible, and gracious, people will seek you out when they need to get something done. You'll be asked to serve on committees, take on special projects, and participate in community activities. People will invite you to parties, take you to lunch, and ask you to join their clubs. Friends will want to hang out with you, tell you their problems, and seek your advice.

All of those things are gratifying in their own way. They are all wonderful compliments. It's a cool thing when people ask you to be part of what they are doing. It's a cool thing when people value your friendship. But the problem is you cannot do everything. You can't do all of the good things that need to be done. You can't even do all of the good things you want to do. You can't be friends with everyone (although you can be friendly to everyone). You can't be all things to all people. You have to choose, because if you don't, you'll be pulled in a million different directions.

It's okay to say "no." In fact, "no" is often the best answer. A reason or excuse is not required. Just say "no." And since you're a gracious person, you'll know how to do that in a nice way.

Much of what you say "no" to will be good things. Much of what you say "no" to might be things you would have liked to have said "yes" to. But there comes a point where you have to draw the line. So where do you draw that pesky line?

✓ It's okay to say "no." In fact, "no" is often the best answer. A reason or excuse is not required. Just say "no." And since you're a gracious person, you'll know how to do that in a nice way.

You have to determine what's most important for you. I would put faith and family at the top of the list. And special friends on that list, too. Work is important, of course. That's why you should devote yourself to work that brings you joy and satisfaction. It's also good to do things just for you. Don't skip the fun stuff. As they say (I have no idea who "they" is), "Life is a journey, enjoy the trip."

One more thing (and this is the tricky part): When making these choices, it's usually not about good and bad. In fact, these choices are easy . . . choose the good, avoid the bad. No problem. With these things I'm talking about, they're all good in their own way and that's what makes it hard. This is a matter of good, better, and best. How can you best use your time and energy? How can you best be you? Choose the best. Choose the excellent. Be confident in that and let the other things go. The greatest threat to excellence is not giving in to the bad. The greatest threat to excellence is settling for the merely good.

Things to Think About:

✓ Where do you draw that pesky line? What's most important for you?

✓ How do you balance being available and generous to others while also being protective of yourself?

✓ When was there a time you felt you were at your best?

✓ Have there been times you were so busy you couldn't do anything well?

BEING YOUR BEST

Whatever you do, work at it with all your heart, as working
for the Lord, not for human masters, since you know that you
will receive an inheritance from the Lord as a reward.
It is the Lord Christ you are serving.
COLOSSIANS 3:23-24

I don't think you can ever do your best. Doing your best
is a process of trying to do your best.
TOWNES VAN ZANDT

Our culture has a lot to say about being the best. Being number one. That's not necessarily a bad thing. In fact, that's at the core of athletic competition. Competing with other people and other teams is all about being the best. Competing with yourself means getting better every day. Giving your best against the best and seeing who comes out on top is rewarding. And, of course, winning is fun.

My school, Auburn University, won the football national championship in 2010. The team had a perfect season . . . 14-0. Cam Newton won the Heisman. It was an amazing year. And it was a terrific year for me, too. I had the opportunity to travel to the title game in Arizona, and since I'm the stadium announcer for Auburn football, I got a national championship ring. I'll never forget how it felt the first time I put it on. It's quite the conversation starter. That ring is so big and sparkly, there's no way to miss it. It's a wonderful thing to be part of a winning team.

The problem is winning gets blown way out of proportion. Not so much by the athletes themselves but by the fans and media. It's odd that the people who get most worked up about being number one (or not) never play a down. Of course, neither did I. I didn't get my ring by playing, I got it by talking, but I'm still proud of my bling.

The truth of being number one is you don't stay there long (if you ever make it at all), and while you're there it seems people are throwing rocks at you trying to knock you down. And maybe a bigger issue is that being ranked inevitably means you're being compared to everyone else rather than standing on your own and being valued for who you are as an individual. Ultimately, life is not a competition.

✓ Being ranked inevitably means you're being compared to everyone else rather than standing on your own and being valued for who you are as an individual. Ultimately, life is not a competition.

I think being the best we can be is a very good thing. But what does it mean to be our best? Some people measure it by accumulations: house, car, clothes . . . rings. Others measure it by achievement: degrees, jobs, promotions . . . championships. It can also be measured by acclaim: notoriety, fame, celebrity . . . screaming fans. All of those things are fine if kept in the proper perspective, although I don't think God is really concerned with any of it. God is much more concerned, I believe, that we do what we are gifted to do and that we give it all we have.

One of my all-time favorite books is *Franny and Zooey* by J.D. Salinger.[4] It's about a family of actors and performers. Franny tells his sister, Zooey, that when performing she should "do it for the fat lady."

In other words, we should perform solely for the joy of that nondescript person in the crowd. And, in some way, that describes everyone. The people in our "audience" may not be enlightened or sophisticated, but they nonetheless deserve our respect and our best effort.

And maybe we're the "fat lady" in a sense. We perform to our standards because they are our standards. We try to be the best . . . not in comparison with others . . . but because we want to be the best we can be for ourselves . . . for the fat lady . . . and (most importantly) for God.

Being our best does not mean we're perfect. It means that in God's grace, we learn, we grow, and we give it all we've got. We should be our best—not for money, or recognition, or position, or ranking. We should be our best because it is the best thing to do. Maybe they don't hand out big, sparkly rings for that, but there's no better feeling in the world.

Things to Think About:

✓ What does it mean to be number one? How is it good? How might it be bad?

✓ Is perfection a destination or a process?

✓ What matters most to you and is it worth sacrificing for?

✓ What are ways we can encourage others and help them be their best?

SUCCESS & SIGNIFICANCE

Jesus called them together and said, 'You know that the rulers
of the Gentiles lord it over them, and their high officials
exercise authority over them. Not so with you. Instead,
whoever wants to be great among you must be your servant,
and whoever wants to be first must be your slave—just as
the Son of Man did not come to be served, but to serve,
and to give his life as a ransom for many.'

MATTHEW 20:25-28

Intentions must mature into commitments if we are to
become persons with definition, with character, with substance.

EUGENE PETERSON

The first line of Rick Warren's book *The Purpose Driven Life*[5] is, "It's not about you." That's a shock to the system, although I have to admit I need to be reminded of that sometimes. It's hard for all of us because we like to think we're the center of the universe to some degree. It crashes against our egos and it certainly contradicts our culture of consumerism and celebrity.

When you look around, it doesn't take long to realize that in America we equate success with stuff. And it's not just any stuff either. It has to be the right stuff—the right car, the right clothes, the right house. Or maybe it means being the center of attention. You know, one of the beautiful people . . . rich and famous . . . the envy of everyone.

Speaking of envy, there is a commercial I've seen for a fertilizer company saying you will be the envy of the neighborhood if you treat your lawn with their miraculous product. Your grass will be so green your neighbors will turn green. Seriously? Success depends on the neighbors being envious? And green grass is all it takes? What a sad place to live. Yeah, that company is selling fertilizer alright . . . manure. I actually have another word in mind, but I'm trying to be polite.

These messages are coming from all directions. And the implication is that if you have all of that stuff or all of those accolades, you'll be successful—you'll be satisfied. In fact, that message is not really implied, it's downright blatant.

I always enjoy talking with students and it's interesting to ask about their plans after college. I am inspired by so many of the students I know, but there are a few who get caught up in the fortune and fame game. Here's an actual conversation:

Ric: What do you want to be when you graduate?

Student: I want to be a news anchor.

Ric: You want to report important stories?

Student: No, I just want to be on TV.

Another actual conversation went like this:

Ric: What do you want to do after graduation?

Student: I want to be successful.

Ric: Be successful at what?

Student: I want to make a lot of money.

It seems they want to be rich and famous just for the sake of being rich and famous. Maybe those students were hoping for some kind of validation to come from wealth and prominence. "Look at how important I am. I'm on TV, I have a blog, I'm on Twitter. See how many times I've been tagged on Facebook." Or "Look at how rich I am. Check out my lifestyle and all of my stuff." Don't buy into that.

If success is based on "stuff" there will never be enough. If it's based on what other people think, the insecurity will never end. There is always a new car or more stylish clothes. There's always a bigger house. Someone else will always have more money—or at least spend it like they do. It's like a drug. The temptation is to want more and more until you can't get enough for your fix. And keep in mind most people telling you these things are trying to sell you something.

What they don't tell you is that success comes from deep down inside. If you're a nobody without wealth and prominence, then you'll be a nobody with it. Success doesn't come from what you have or who is watching. Success comes from who you are and the relationships you have with other people. And there is no greater success at all than being significant in someone else's life.

✓ What they don't tell you is that success comes from deep down inside. If you're a nobody without that stuff, then you'll be a nobody with it. Success doesn't come from what you have or who is watching. Success comes from who you are and how you impact the lives of other people.

Think about five people you know who have influenced your life (other than your parents). I mean people you really know and have a real-life human connection with, not just someone you know about. I'm pretty sure you remember them now because they cared for you and loved you in some special way. They probably weren't famous, and they may—or may not—have been successful in that position, power, and big money kind of way. And the fact of the matter is you probably don't really care one way or the other because that was not the most important thing. But they were significant. You are a better person for having known them. You are a better person because they cared for you and loved you.

The amazing thing is you can be just as significant for someone you know. You have the opportunity to be as significant for someone as those people were for you. That's pretty heady stuff. You won't become rich and famous for it. There is no reality show for that. No one will know . . . other than the one whose life you have changed.

Things to Think About:

✓ How do you define success? What does it mean to be successful in life?

✓ What's the danger of allowing others to define success for us?

✓ How does envy work as an advertising tool? Is it possible for a commercial to make a person feel empty so that emptiness can be filled with their product?

✓ Name someone (other than your parents) who had an impact on your life. What did they do for you? How did they do it?

✓ Have you considered that you may be impacting someone now? What are things you can do now that may be significant to someone else?

REPUTATION & CHARACTER

Jesus and his disciples went on to the villages around Caesarea
Philippi. On the way he asked them, 'Who do people say I am?'
MARK 8:27

Many a man's reputation would not know his character
if they met on the street.
ELBERT HUBBARD

You cannot control your reputation. What I mean is you cannot control what other people think of you. You can, however, make good decisions that will enhance your reputation. If you're honest, wise, considerate, and keep good company, people will likely think well of you.

The people you surround yourself with go a long way in impacting your reputation. It works in two ways: First, you will be known by the company you keep. That means your reputation will be connected to their reputations (both good and bad). It's just human nature to assume you would be the same kind of person as the people with whom you spend time. You know the old saying, "birds of a feather flock together." That may be a stereotype, but always remember stereotypes are based on observation and carry a kernel of truth. And the fact of the matter is we are greatly influenced by the people around us. Hang out with good people and the good will rub off on you. You'll be more likely to make good decisions with their good influence. Hang out with "not so good" people and the "not so good" will rub off. They make it easy for you to make bad decisions . . . although it's always your decision, not theirs.

Unfortunately, in some circumstances people will think what they want to think no matter how "clean" you're living. As you know, some people gossip, some people lie. There are those who would rather tear down than build up. That's why you can only influence your reputation and not control it. You just can't control what people think or say, but you can control your character.

 Reputation may be what people say you are, but character is who you truly are. Character is who you are when no one is looking.

Reputation may be what people say you are, but character is who you truly are. Character is who you are when no one is looking. Character is between you and God—nobody else.

The odd thing is, there are people with good reputations who are not people of good character. They may have some of the people fooled, but they can't fool themselves. They know who they are. They know it when they lie in bed at night and they know it when they look in the mirror in the morning.

Of course, it works the other way too. People of strong character do not always enjoy the best reputations. If you think about it, Jesus' reputation among the leaders of his day was as bad as it gets. It was so bad they crucified him. But you and I know that no one could be of stronger character. Jesus knew it was between him and God—nobody else.

One more thing: Never allow other people to make you into something you are not. Respond based on who you are—your character—not who they are or who they expect you to be. Don't let them suck you in and pull you down to their level.

67

Things to Think About:

✓ What is the difference to you between reputation and character?

✓ A good reputation can be constructed over time. How do you construct good character?

✓ Why do you think a person of high character will inevitably suffer attacks on his or her reputation?

PRIVATE & SECRET

For there is nothing hidden that will not be disclosed, and nothing concealed that will not be known or brought out into the open.

LUKE 8:17

Never doubt in the dark what God told you in the light.

V. RAYMOND EDMAN

Before I leave for work each morning, I spend time addressing my personal concerns. You know, all of that cleaning and shining we do as we get ready for the day ahead. Much of that is done behind closed doors, even though it's all quite ordinary and proper. In fact, it's something we all do and it's something we all know we all do; yet it's private. Our lives are filled with such personal and intimate moments. They are not for the whole world to see but neither are they hidden.

Then there are the hidden things. When we don't want anyone to know what we're up to, when we want to keep things out of sight, that's a bad sign. If we're thinking of ways to keep "it" a secret (as opposed to private), that's a good indication we don't need to be doing "it." If we don't want our spouse to know, our best friends to know, God to know, we should drop "it" and move on to better things. It says something about our motivations if we want to keep things hidden from the people we care the most about . . . and who care the most about us.

The old ethics check called "the front page test" is a helpful guide. Ask yourself how you would feel if your actions were printed on the front page of the local newspaper. To make it a little more current, maybe we should rename it "the Twitter test," but you get the idea.

 It says something about our motivations if we want to keep things hidden from the people we care the most about . . . and who care the most about us.

Luke 8:17 says, "For there is nothing hidden that will not be disclosed, and nothing concealed that will not be known or brought out into the open." I've never read that verse as a threat. I just think it's our reality. Most everything comes out eventually and that's especially true in today's electronic world. It's not just about newspapers, radio, or television. Everyone, it seems, is posting in some way. Gossip travels at the speed of light.

Even though it's tough to keep secrets, it's not impossible, so that raises a more important issue . . . integrity. What is ultimately important is not the ability to keep secrets but the desire to make wise choices you have no need to hide.

Things to Think About:

✓ Why is it a bad sign if we want to keep something secret (as opposed to private)?

✓ Do you agree that most every secret eventually comes out?

✓ How do you relate to friends who suddenly become secretive? How do you balance respecting a friend's privacy and being concerned with decisions they are making?

WHAT WAS I THINKING?

The Lord makes firm the steps of the one who delights
in him; though he may stumble, he will not fall,
for the Lord upholds him with his hand.
PSALM 37:23-24

I may not yet be the man I should be or the man,
with Christ's help, I someday will be—
but thank God I'm not the man I used to be.
MARTIN LUTHER KING, JR.

Now that you're leaving home, you'll be stepping into a new life in a new world. You'll be living on your own, meeting new people, trying new things. You'll take on more responsibility and make more decisions as you become an independent adult.

The problem is there is no magic day when "adult" suddenly happens (I'm still waiting for my magic day). It's a long, slow process. Nevertheless, there is a time when you have to leave the nest—even if you're not very good at flying.

Bumps and bruises along the way are inevitable. You'll try new things . . . many of them will be good and you'll stick with them. You'll try new things . . . many of them will be pretty bad and you'll move on. You'll even try some new things . . . that may make you shudder when you look back at them. You'll certainly have some of those "what was I thinking?" moments. I hope they are few and far between, but they'll be there.

72

While all of our experiences change us in some way, my hope is your "what was I thinking?" moments are not life changing in a catastrophic or unalterable way. The reality is some decisions impact the rest of our lives. Some things (like a drunk-driving car crash) you may never fully recover from.

 You are not defined by any one moment. Your character is not determined by any one choice. Never let other people label you. More important, don't ever label yourself.

But having said that, let me say this . . . you are not defined by any one moment. Your character is not determined by any one choice. Never let other people label you. More important, don't ever label yourself. In fact, if you're asking yourself "what was I thinking?" type questions, it shows you know something is wrong. It shows you are aware of what was and what can be. Live, learn, grow, and then move on. And always remember the miracle of grace is that good things can come from bad circumstances.

Things to Think About:

✓ Have you thought about leaving the nest? How does that excite you? Does it frighten you in any way (and it's okay if it does because it's a big step in life)?

✓ What decisions have you made that have had a major impact on your life?

✓ How have you experienced the miracle of grace? How have you seen good things come from bad circumstances?

✓ How do you respond when someone you know is making bad decisions? What's the difference between being meddlesome and concerned?

THE DEMON ALCOHOL

Wine is a mocker and beer a brawler;
whoever is led astray by them is not wise.
PROVERBS 20:1

When I get honest, I admit I am a bundle of paradoxes.
I believe and I doubt, I hope and get discouraged, I love and I
hate, I feel bad about feeling good, I feel guilty about not feeling
guilty. I am trusting and suspicious. I am honest and I still
play games. Aristotle said I am a rational animal; I say I am
an angel with an incredible capacity for beer.
BRENNAN MANNING

It would be easy for me to say to you, "Don't drink." Of course, I've
been known to have a cold drink or two on occasion so that would
be rather hypocritical. And, to be honest, there have been times when
I've had more than I should have. Having said that, here are a few
things to keep in mind.

If you're under twenty-one, you are legally underage. I must admit,
I think it's silly that the legal drinking age in this country is twenty-
one. It seems to me that if you are old enough to go to war, vote, get
married, and have children you should be old enough to buy a drink. I
certainly understand drunk driving is a problem among young people
(and way too many older people as well). However, there is no good
fairy who mysteriously appears on your twenty-first birthday to sprin-
kle maturity dust on your head. There is nothing magic about that day

75

to suddenly make you all grown up. I've met a few eighteen-year-olds who are more mature than some forty-year-olds I know. Nevertheless, the legal age is twenty-one, so you would be breaking the law. If you get caught, you'll have to deal with it.

Remember too, there is a big difference between having a drink or two and tying one on . . . being three sheets to the wind . . . getting hammered, blasted, or toasted. Binge drinking is considered to be five or more drinks in one sitting (I think standing up counts, too). Some people think it's cool to out-drink everyone in the room. They like to brag about how many beers they've had. Or how they can hold their liquor. Believe me, throwing up, falling down, and passing out are not cool.

I guarantee you there will come a night when some moron will say you're a wimp/chicken/baby if you don't have a drink . . . or twelve. That's just stupid. You will be much more strong/brave/mature by being true to yourself rather than going along with the crowd.

Some people do dumb things when they get drunk and say "the alcohol made me do it." No. They did it. It is true that alcohol impairs our judgment and that people may do things when drunk they would not do otherwise, but that's no excuse. When we drink, we're accountable. It's our choice to drink so we're responsible for the results—no matter what.

We often don't want to admit it, but alcohol is a drug . . . just like marijuana is a drug . . . and Ritalin . . . OxyContin . . . cocaine . . . meth . . . the list just keeps going. Is marijuana worse than alcohol? I'm not convinced it is. Others on the list certainly can be worse and some are absolutely worse. And the fact is marijuana, prescription drugs (when you don't have the prescription) and all of the others are illegal. You can go to jail. And for many people, using one (including alcohol) leads to other things . . . very frightening things.

I think there is a deeper issue here though. Many people use drugs to escape. And quite often those drugs are prescribed by a doctor or even sold over the counter. Our medicine cabinets are filled with drugs for depression, anxiety, stress, tension, and hyperactivity. We take drugs to put us to sleep and drugs to wake us up. Certainly there are people with legitimate problems who require the help of medicine. But it seems to me so much of our drug use in this country—legal and illegal, prescribed and over-the-counter, socially acceptable or not—is the result of lifestyle issues. If we are so stressed out, worked up, and run down we need drugs to make us right, something is wrong.

 If we are so stressed out, worked up and run down we need drugs to make us right, something is wrong.

So what's the bottom line of this little piece of advice? If you are not yet twenty-one, it would be better if you did not drink. If you do, you are responsible for whatever happens. Don't drink and drive and don't ever ride in the car with someone who has been drinking. Call a cab. Call a friend. Call your parents to come get you. If you wake them up in the middle of the night, they might be a little irritable, but it won't be anything compared to how irritable they will be if they find out you didn't call when you should have. They love you more than they'll be mad at you . . . although you might not be able to tell it at the time.

Here's something else to keep in mind. I wish life was not this way, but it is. Don't ever accept a drink from a person you don't know, and even be careful accepting drinks from people you do know. Don't ever set your drink down. Hold it. It's just too easy for someone to put something in your drink. Maybe drink only out of a bottle—I mean a beer or wine cooler bottle . . . if you're drinking out of a liquor bottle, it's going to be a bad night. I think it would be even better if you drank out of a child's "sippy" cup, but I admit that would look a little strange. If you go out on the town, go with a friend. Stay together and look out for each other.

Never forget there are people who will take advantage of you. There are people who will harm you. I believe those people are the exception rather than the rule, but they are there nonetheless. And it only takes one to alter your life.

Things to Think About:

✓ We must pass a test to drive, should there be a drinking test?

✓ Who could you call if you needed a ride home?

✓ When does responsible drinking become irresponsible? Is responsible drinking an oxymoron?

✓ How do you respond to someone who has had too much to drink? What if it becomes a regular occurrence?

IT'S YOUR CHOICE

Your word is a lamp for my feet, a light on my path.
PSALM 119:105

We are in constant danger of being not actors in the drama of our
lives but reactors, to go where the world takes us, to drift with
whatever current happens to be running strongest.
FREDERICK BUECHNER

Life is not so much about what happens to you as it is about how
you react to what happens to you. And more important, it's about
steps you take to make your life a good one.

Life isn't fair. Don't expect it to be. It's different for everybody. You'll see people who are richer, poorer, healthier, sicker, taller,
shorter, faster, and slower than you. Some will be smarter. Some folks
are not as smart as you. And some will have severe problems. Some
people have the support of loving families (I hope that is true for you
. . . although during your early teen years you may have thought you
were being raised by a pack of morons). Some come from absolutely
horrible situations where there is no love and no support.

Even if you've had a good start, you won't know what the future
holds. Now, I don't want to come across as a little black rain cloud.
I'm not saying "LOOK OUT! Bad times are coming." However, it's
a fact that everyone faces disappointments in life and some people
face real tragedies. You have to decide how to react to what life brings
you. You can be positive or negative. You can dwell on the past or

work toward the future. You can wallow in self-pity or grow from the experience. It's up to you.

The bottom line of all of this advice is you have to buy into it on your own. No one can do it for you. Not me. Not your parents. Not your friends. Just you. Oh, sure, you will be influenced by other people. You may even let other people do the thinking for you but even abdication is a choice. You will decide what you will do. You will decide how you will live.

Always be honest with yourself and know you can't hide from yourself, although a lot of people try. They attempt to fool themselves into thinking they're something other than what they truly are, but it doesn't work. Deep down inside they know, and that subconscious knowledge can bubble up in some crazy ways. And the strange thing is, what they're trying to fool themselves about can be either positive or negative.

Refusing to see the negative is not hard to understand. There are just some people who refuse to face the facts (and I'm sure I have my moments as well). It's like if they ignore it, it will go away. Or if they refuse to acknowledge it, then it can't be real. Oh, it's real and it's not going away on its own.

The other side of that is there are people who refuse to acknowledge the positive. They refuse to see they have a lot going for them. They refuse to see the potential and to recognize the value in themselves. I think that's worse. Sure, we all have our problems. We all have our negatives. But it's also true that everyone matters. Everyone has something to contribute, something to offer.

I've always been interested in how different people see the world in different ways. Here's what I mean: There are some people who have had pretty easy lives and they have a warm, fuzzy view of the world. That's not hard to understand. There are other people who have lived tough lives and they develop a cold, hard view of the world. That's not hard to understand either.

But then, there are those people who have had pretty good lives, yet they always focus on the negative. Things have been pretty darn good, but they can only see the bad. That's fascinating . . . and sad.

 Life is not so much about what happens to you as it is about how you react to what happens to you.

The ones who truly fascinate me and even inspire me are those people who have had hard lives (sometimes tragic) yet they always see the light at the end of the tunnel, the flower pushing through the concrete, the rainbow after the storm (please insert favorite cheesy cliché here). You know what I mean. Things have been tough, but they choose joy. If the bad outnumbers the good ten to one, they choose the one. And that's not refusing to see reality either. That's not sticking their heads in the sand (the cliché count now stands at four). It's dealing with what comes their way and in the end choosing joy. That is very cool. I want to be like that.

It is said you are the sum total of your life's experiences (cliché five). You are what you are now because of everything that has happened to you up to this point. Build on your successes and learn from your shortcomings. Life is a journey not a destination (cliché six but nevertheless true). Some days you walk along the beach or through the mountains and the scenery is wonderful. Other days it seems you're trudging through the desert and it will never end. Always keep a good map and true compass. Put yourself on the right path and when you get lost, turn around. Go back to the good trail. Enjoy the trip. You never know what's over the next hill.

Things to Think About:

✓ In what ways do people react to what comes their way?

✓ How do you tend to react? Are you an optimist or pessimist? If you're a "glass half-empty" type person, do you think it's possible to change your perspective?

✓ How do the decisions we make now impact what is to come?

ALWAYS CONNECTED

At daybreak, Jesus went out to a solitary place. The people
were looking for him and when they came to where he was,
they tried to keep him from leaving them.

LUKE 4:42

Look at the world and think about a catastrophic disaster where
the cell phone towers went dead. How would you ever be able
to 'TEXT' your next door neighbor to see if they were okay?

STANLEY VICTOR PASKAVICH

I once asked my students what technology they would rather do
without if they had the power to make it go away. The number one
response was texting. A close second was social media. And cell
phones (the talking function) came in third. So I asked why they
didn't just refuse to use it. Why not stop texting, tweeting, posting,
and answering? They can't. And that, they said, is the problem . . .
even though they would like to turn everything off, it has become virtually impossible. The pressure to be always connected is too strong.

We are expected to be connected at all times, in all circumstances,
and that demand comes from all directions. Friends get mad when we
don't immediately return a text. The boss expects us to be available for
a quick call or email at night and on the weekend. And parents get
worried when their child doesn't answer a call, even if they are in class,
at work, or on a date . . . or maybe just out on the town having a little
late-night fun.

Having said all that, let me also say I'm (mostly) glad to have a smart phone (and tablet) and all the apps that go with it. I'm certainly no Luddite. I text and tweet and make Facebook posts, too. I even have actual conversations on my phone. New technology can be a wonderful tool (and you know that better than I do), but for all the conveniences technology offers, it causes at least as many problems.

 We are expected to be connected at all times, in all circumstances, and that demand comes from all directions.

The greatest problem with technology, in my opinion, is we focus so much on our devices we lose the ability to connect with people who are physically with us. We're so electronically in-touch, we lose the human touch. I can't count the number of times I've walked into a room full of people only to see everyone connected electronically and disconnected personally. No one was talking. Or the times I've been in a meeting where the people in the group were much more focused on what they might be missing "out there" rather than what was going on "in here." No one was paying attention. I've even seen couples at dinner, obviously on a date, who spent the entire evening on their phones. I think it's safe to assume they weren't texting each other.

It's easy to get caught up in *keeping up*, where we're continually *checking in* to make sure we're never *missing out*, falling victim to the "tyranny of the urgent." The tyranny of the urgent is when we allow outside influences (like emails, texts, tweets, posts, and "breaking" news) to convince us some issue is an emergency when it really isn't. It's focusing on the "squeaky wheel" just because it squeaks, not because it truly matters. That noise is all around us (even though most of it is completely inconsequential), distracting us from what matters most . . . real people and real relationships.

Sending a text is fine. Having a face-to-face conversation (when that's possible, and it frequently is) is richer. Posting a picture on Facebook is a convenient way to let your friends know what you're up to. Posting a contrived life in order to rack-up "likes" is tragic. Occasionally checking email or news headlines to stay informed is not a problem. Constantly surfing your apps while ignoring family and friends demonstrates a troubling lack of priorities. You get the idea.

Yes, I do understand "real relationships" can be shared through technology, and that's a very good thing, but the reality is relationships frequently suffer because of technology . . . not to mention our own peace of mind and well-being suffering as well.

That's really what I'm getting at. It's good to be connected, but make sure you stay connected in the most important way . . . as one human being with another . . . seeing, talking, hearing, and touching (in socially approved ways, of course).

It's okay to silence the ringer, log-off, and power down. I would encourage you to find a block of time each week to be disconnected from technology and intentionally connected with the most important people in your life . . . and with yourself. . . and with God. Maybe even try a twenty-four hour technology-free day. You'll be amazed what it will do for you . . . and it'll freak out your friends, too.

Use technology, don't let it use you. I have to go . . . I just got a text.

Things to Think About:

✓ What technology would you rather do without if you had the power to make it go away?

✓ In what ways do you feel pressured to be connected? Does the most pressure come from friends, family, or work? Or is it all three?

✓ Would you consider silencing the ringer, logging off, and powering down for twenty-four hours? What do you think would happen? Would you need to warn people before you did it?

TELEVISION

Walk with the wise and become wise,
for a companion of fools suffers harm.
PROVERBS 13:20

Television is the first truly democratic culture—the first culture
available to everybody and entirely governed by what the
people want. The most terrifying thing is what people do want.
CLIVE BARNES

Television will suck the brains out of your head. Or at least it
can, if you let it. According to the Nielsen Company (the TV
ratings people), the average person watches more than four and
one-half hours of television each day. Watching TV (along with
other forms of video) is the number one leisure time activity. And for
many families, TV's are everywhere . . . in the den, in the bedroom,
in the kitchen, and even in the bathroom (I know those people inside
the TV can't see me in the bathroom, but I still think it's creepy).

And that's just in the house. It's virtually impossible to go any-
where and not be exposed to television. Just try finding a restaurant
that doesn't have a television flashing and blaring . . . even swanky
restaurants (and I wouldn't even include sports bars in this list because
sports television is what they are designed for). Most waiting rooms
have televisions. Check-out lines and airport boarding areas have them,
too. I've seen televisions in bookstores and libraries.

And that's not all. We have "TV" on our smart phones, tablets, and laptops, so wherever we go, we take television with us. We watch so much television in so many places it begins to take over . . . bombarding us with never-ending noise and images . . . never-ending commercials. It's as if we're addicted to television. We watch it wherever and whenever. We turn it on when we first wake up in the morning and fall asleep by the glow of the screen at night. We may even plan our lives around television. It seems to me something's wrong when TV becomes the focus of our lives.

I once overheard a conversation a group of people at work were having about "what we did last night." One woman in the group said, "My husband and I were home last night and we were flipping through the TV guide. We couldn't find anything we wanted to watch, so we just had to watch what was on." It's like her whole view of life was that you go to work . . . go home and spend the evening watching television. My guess is the only difference on the weekend was that they didn't go to work. That's frightening.

Having said all of that, I must also say television is not all bad. In fact, there are times it can be quite good, so it's not fair for people (including me) to say television is responsible for everything that is wrong in our world. The fact of the matter is we are not forced to watch (even when we're held captive in a waiting room). I've never seen a television without a channel changer and I've never seen a television without an on/off switch. And if all else fails, unplug the damn thing.

Now I agree there are some serious social issues we need to address and television is a factor. And I believe television programmers and advertisers have a moral and ethical responsibility to the community. We all do. We're all responsible for our actions . . . both as providers and consumers.

Ultimately, however, it's not the TV's fault. When it comes right down to it, television is nothing more than an appliance like a toaster or an iron. In fact, I think it's most like a refrigerator.

When you buy a refrigerator, it arrives at your house empty (well . . . it doesn't actually "arrive," it's delivered by a couple of really big, strong guys). You then have to go out to the grocery store for food to stock it—to fill it up. You can choose to fill the refrigerator with healthy foods like fish and milk and broccoli. Or you can go for other things like bacon and beer and ice cream.

Wouldn't it be cool to have a magic refrigerator that comes fully stocked? Every time you open the door it's filled with anything and everything you could imagine. Well, television is like that magic refrigerator.

Wouldn't it be cool to have a magic refrigerator that comes fully stocked? Every time you open the door it's filled with anything and everything you could imagine. Well, television is like that magic refrigerator. When you buy a TV it comes fully stocked, so there's no going to the store. And it stays that way. Any time and every time you turn it on. All day. All night. All weekend. Just plug it in, connect the cable, and suddenly your television is full and ready to watch . . . ready for your brain to eat.

When you push the button and stare into your television (which is a lot like opening the door and staring into your magic refrigerator), you'll find there's some good stuff in there and some not so good stuff, too. It seems to me the secret to this appliance is what and how much "food" you choose to take out of it. In other words, what you feed your brain and how much you feed it. There is nothing wrong with a snack now and then. A little junk food is fine. Ice cream tastes great, but if you eat it all the time, it will make you sick. A little junk TV is okay, but if you watch too much TV (even good TV), it will also make you sick.

There is one big difference between a refrigerator and television though. If you leave food in the refrigerator too long it goes bad and you have to throw it out. You know, the old casserole that gets pushed into the back for a couple of weeks and turns green and fuzzy. Nobody would eat that green fuzzy stuff. It would make you sick.

TV has green fuzzy stuff, too. There's some pretty nasty stuff in there. And the weird thing is, people who would never eat the green fuzzy stuff in the refrigerator will turn on the TV and feed those green fuzzy shows to their brains. It will make you sick.

So what's important is how (and how much) we use it . . . the choices we make. It's perfectly fine to watch a little TV. Enjoy some of the good stuff. And a junky treat once in a while, too . . . just not the green fuzzy stuff.

One other thing to keep in mind is that television is a business. It exists to make money. Again, that's not to say it's all bad. Stations can be profitable and good corporate citizens at the same time. But always remember, they are trying to sell you something. It's usually a product, or it could be an idea or point of view. Can you trust television? Maybe, maybe not. Here's a warning sign . . . if they keep telling you how trustworthy, fair, and dependable they are, it's a pretty good sign they're not.

Things to Think About:

✓ How much television do you watch? Consider keeping a week-long log of when and what you're watching. You might be surprised.

✓ How does television impact the people you live with? Is it something you do together or does it separate you from each other?

✓ Are you a better person or a better family for having spent time with that program?

READING

Blessed are those who find wisdom, those who gain
understanding, for she is more profitable than silver and yields
better returns than gold.
PROVERBS 3:13-14

I find television very educating. Every time somebody turns on the
set, I go into the other room and read a book.
GROUCHO MARX

Martin Tupper said, "A good book is the best of friends, the same today and forever."[6] A book always sits ready and waiting. It provides wonderful companionship. It is dependable and welcoming. Exciting. Melancholy. Happy. Aggravating. With some books I enjoy their company so much I hate to see our time together growing short as my bookmark moves closer to the last page. And then there are those books where a short visit is the best visit. With others, we meet again and again, and I learn more about these friends each time we sit down together.

Never stop reading. Surround yourself with books. You will find great wisdom there and, at times, some foolishness, too. Read critically and always remember that an idea being set down on paper does not make it inherently worthwhile or true (and that certainly applies to this book). Books are like people in many ways. Associate with those that make you a better person for having known them. Read books that expand your mind and touch your soul. And sometimes read just for the fun of it.

When I am invited to someone's home I always notice his or her books. Who do they read? What do they read? It's a great opportunity for conversation and to find a book-sharing friend. Books recommended by friends are some of the best I've ever read.

Books will teach you, challenge you, entertain you. Books will help you grow. You will find them to be wonderful companions.

✓ Books are like people in many ways. Associate with those that make you a better person for having known them. Read books that expand your mind and touch your soul. And sometimes read just for the fun of it.

A few years ago, my lovely wife, Carole, and I decided to read all of the Pulitzer Prize winning fiction novels from the time we were born (and since she is two years older than me, she had more reading to do . . . I'm going to pay for that one). We thought it would be a good way to expand our reading list and try new things. Some books I had already read but most I had not. And many I hadn't read, I probably would never have tried. All the books were good (okay, there was one I thought was awful) and some were marvelous. It has been a wonderful experience. Now that Carole and I are caught up, we look forward to April each year when the new winner is announced.

Here are a few of my all-time favorite books. Some were Pulitzer winners, most were not. My list is always changing and growing, so here's what it looks like today (in no particular order) . . .

War and Peace, Leo Tolstoy
A Prayer for Owen Meaney, John Irving
Hannah Coulter, Wendell Berry
Light in August, William Faulkner

The Karamazov Brothers, Fyodor Dostoevsky
The Great Gatsby, F. Scott Fitzgerald
In the Heart of the Sea, Nathaniel Philbrick
Traveling Mercies, Anne Lamott
Searching for God Knows What, Donald Miller
What's So Amazing About Grace, Philip Yancey
The Cost of Discipleship, Dietrich Bonheoffer
The Optimist's Daughter, Eudora Welty
Isaac's Storm, Erik Larson
A Christmas Memory, Truman Capote
Franny and Zooey, J.D. Salinger
Gilead, Marilynne Robinson
Beloved, Toni Morrison
The Whisper of the River, Ferrol Sams
An Altar in the World, Barbara Brown Taylor

Things to Think About:

✓ What is your favorite book? Why? What types of books do you enjoy?

✓ What book do you most often recommend or give as a gift?

✓ Do you find time to read or make time to read?

SERENDIPITY

And we know that in all things God works for the good of those
who love him, who have been called according to his purpose.
ROMANS 8:28

I know nothing, except what everyone knows—
if there when Grace dances, I should dance.
W.H. AUDEN

'm a firm believer in serendipity, fortuitous moments that make life sweeter. Some people call it luck, but I'm not so sure. I don't really believe in luck. It seems to me luck is just something that happens to you. It may be good and it could be bad.

Serendipity, on the other hand, is always a good thing. It is unexpected good fortune. And since it's unexpected, you can't really go looking for it, but you can put yourself in the right position so it can find you. Serendipity is more about putting yourself in the right frame of mind than putting yourself in the right place. It's about emotional geography much more than physical geography.

There have been occasions where I have attempted to create the perfect date or perfect vacation or perfect party. And I've discovered it's impossible. If you expect perfection, you're doomed to fail. It's just not going to happen. Then you find yourself focusing on what goes wrong rather than what goes right. You set yourself up to fret over the shortcomings. And if by some miracle things go exactly as you plan, you won't really enjoy it because you'll be a nervous wreck. All you've done is meet expectations and there is no real joy in that. The wonderful thing about serendipity is oftentimes the surprise is much better than the original plan.

December 31, 1999 . . . we were having a "Year 2000" New Year's Eve party at our house. There were three couples with their kids, plus my lovely wife, Carole, our wonderful son, Harry, and me. We had invited another couple and their children, but they said they wanted a "special" dinner for Y2K. They weren't snooty about it, they just wanted something more elegant for the occasion . . . more about that later.

✓ Serendipity is more about putting yourself in the right frame of mind than putting yourself in the right place. It's about emotional geography much more than physical geography.

The kids at our party were somewhere between the ages of three and eight, so for dinner we set them up with pizza and other fun foods. For the grown-ups we had steak and lobster (seemed pretty "special" to me) . . . and that's where serendipity came into the picture.

I grilled the steaks and steamed the lobsters (fortunately for me, I had a college friend from Boston who taught me how). The kids were partying at the kids' table and the adults sat down around the dining room table (we even used the fancy china). I said the blessing (Lord, make us thankful for these and all our blessings, we ask in Christ's name, amen). And then . . . we had nothing for cracking open the lobsters. I had absolutely forgotten to buy shell crackers. So I went out to the tool shed and got pliers . . . channel locks . . . vice grips . . . even hammers . . . just about any tool we could use to crack those things open. It was pretty darn funny. As we were eating, I held up my channel locks (covered in lobster juice) and said, "This is just like eating at Red Lobster.™" To which my friend Eric said, "It's more like eating at Red-Neck Lobster." Serendipity is a wonderful thing.

A few days later I bumped into the other couple and asked how their night had gone. Let's just say things didn't turn out the way they planned. In that "elegant" setting, the parents were tense and demanding and the kids were bored and restless. Once things started going wrong, the "perfect" evening was ruined.

Please understand, I'm not telling this story to make them look bad. They are wonderful people and they wanted to do something special for their family. That's always a good thing. But I think their expectations were too high and they lost focus of the most important thing.

Expectations and focus are what serendipity is all about. Expect good things, even in challenging times. Focus on good things, especially in challenging times. Be open to the sweet moments of life and share them with the people you love. The blessing of serendipity is you will find yourself basking in those wonderful moments of grace that are a great prize, and surprise, of life.

Things to Think About:

✓ Have you ever had something go wrong and then turn out even better than you expected?

✓ What is emotional geography?

✓ There is nothing wrong with planning. In fact, good planning can be very important. So how do you make good plans while still leaving the door open for serendipity?

I NEVER THOUGHT IT WOULD COME TO THIS

So do not fear, for I am with you; do not be dismayed,
for I am your God. I will strengthen you and help you;
I will uphold you with my righteous right hand.
ISAIAH 41:10

Write it on your heart that each day is the best day in the year.
RALPH WALDO EMERSON

I had a student once who came to my office to talk about things. She had made a bad grade on an exam and wanted to know what had gone wrong. She also wanted to talk about the internship she would be required to complete before graduating.

I have to say, it was not a good conversation. It just didn't go well. She didn't like what I said about her exam (I was nice about it, but she had done a poor job). Plus, she was frustrated about the idea of the internship. It wasn't so much that our meeting was unpleasant, it's just everything about it was rather awkward and uncomfortable. And it was pretty obvious she had something else on her mind.

Then she got real quiet. I noticed her eyes filled with tears . . . and then the tears spilled over (fortunately, I keep a box of tissues handy for just such an emergency). I asked her what was wrong and the conversation went something like this:

Student: I never thought it would come to this.

Me: Never thought it would come to what?

Student: I just never thought it would come to this.

Me: This what?

Student: I never thought I would have to graduate and get a job.

Me: What did you think would happen?

Student: I don't know. I just never thought this would happen.

She loved being in college. She was a majorette, pretty and very popular. She was having the time of her life. And one day it hit her that it had indeed come to this . . . college was coming to an end . . . it was time to move on to the next thing.

 Enjoy every moment for what it is. Appreciate what you have when you have it because things are going to change. That is life, and life is lived right here, right now.

When you first walk onto your college campus, graduation can seem a million miles away. It's really not. Those four years pass by in the proverbial twinkling of an eye. Just a "couple" of years ago, I was in college myself it seems.

And that's true with most other things in life. When you first go to work, it's like you'll never move up in the ranks. When you first get married, you think you'll live together forever. When your children are born, it seems your kids will always be kids (especially when they're screaming in the middle of the night). Yet it all goes by so much faster than you could ever imagine.

Enjoy every moment for what it is. Appreciate what you have when you have it because things are going to change. That is life, and life is lived right here, right now.

There's an old saying that is very true . . . time waits for no man (or woman). Time does indeed march on . . . that's another old saying that's true. It will always come to this.

Things to Think About:

✓ Do you remember when it seemed Christmas would never come? Now look back on all the Christmases that have come . . . and gone. Doesn't it all seem so fast? Does the passing of your high school years seem just as fast?

✓ Are you excited about your new life or does it seem like something you have to fight your way through?

✓ Why does time seem so much shorter in reflection than it does in anticipation?

LOVE

DATING

So Jacob served seven years to get Rachel, but they seemed like
only a few days to him because of his love for her.
GENESIS 29:20

Love is like playing the piano. First you must learn to play by the
rules, then you must forget the rules and play from your heart.
ANONYMOUS

The most important lesson I learned about dating is that girls were just as afraid of me as I was of them. And that's an amazing thing because I was scared to death. So now we know . . . we are all equally terrified of each other.

Just imagine you're sitting in Biology 101. Across the classroom you see Taylor Jordan Casey. If you're from the South, that student is named Taylor-Jordan Casey (double first name). If you're from the North or West, the name is Taylor Jordan-Casey (hyphenated last name). Nevertheless, please notice the non-gender-specific name used for the purposes of our discussion.

Anyway, there sits TJC three rows over . . . looking good with beautiful eyes and a big smile. It makes your stomach jump and you get all tingly just thinking about it. That's somebody you want to meet.

Now what? Say hello and see what happens. Believe me, I understand the fear of rejection is always tough and the fact of the matter is it never gets easy. However, there will come a point where you'll just have to work up the courage to strike up a conversation. What if it bombs? Oh well. It's going to happen sooner or later. That's okay. You'll hear "not interested" a lot of times in your life. That's just the way it goes. The trick is to make sure you find a way to meet that special someone who catches your eye so they will have the opportunity to say yes. You might be surprised to find that TJC had been studying your biology all along.

So let's say you and TJC decide to do something together. Relax and have a good time. It seems to me there are two reasons for dating. One is to find someone to marry (and that may not be as far down the road as you think . . . I was twenty-three when my lovely wife, Carole, and I got married). The other is to find someone you enjoy spending time with (and that may very well be the person you marry). The point is have fun and be yourself.

The first date Carole and I had really wasn't a date at all. I thought she would be fun to hang out with, so one day I asked if she wanted to do something after work (we worked at a radio station together—I was the morning DJ and she was the sales manager). We ended up going to a playground and swinging on the tire swing (I'm such a big spender). There was no pressure. No formal date. Just two people talking and enjoying each other's company.

Keep in mind Carole and I dated other people before we met each other. You and your spouse-to-be (whomever and wherever that person is) will date other people, too. It may be you go out with someone a few times and it turns into something special. Or maybe it doesn't turn into that special thing, but you've found a new friend. And sometimes two people discover they are not cut out for each other so you each go your own way. That's okay, too. Let it be what it is. If you find that special someone, you'll know. If not, you'll know when it's time to move on.

Never feel pressured to date and never let yourself think the clock is ticking. Some people have it in their minds they have to be married by a certain age. I know plenty of college students (both guys and girls) who think they have to be engaged by graduation. Dating gets really frantic for them during the spring of their senior year. In a weird way it's like last-minute shopping on Christmas Eve. Never settle on a gift or a spouse just because you're running out of time. You can't return a spouse the way you can return a sweater.

✓ It may be you go out with someone a few times and it turns into something special. Or maybe it doesn't turn into that special thing, but you've found a new friend. And sometimes two people discover they are not cut out for each other so you each go your own way. That's okay, too. Let it be what it is.

Just as bad is the idea of marrying the "right" person from the "right" family with the "right" prospects. This isn't about making a business deal, and it's certainly not about two kings forming an alliance by having their prince and princess allied in marriage. You don't have to study much history to know how disastrous that could be. That's just crazy.

And speaking of crazy . . . some people are nuts. Run away from crazy people. I have to say I knew some "unique" women in my time. But to be fair, I have to admit women have it much worse than men when it comes to dating. Not only can men be just as "unique," we are often times much worse . . . possessive, jealous, insecure, libidinous, even violent. There is absolutely no excuse for that. Not ever.

Always be respectful. Always be honorable. Be honest. Don't play games. And expect the same from your friend. I've known couples who have made each other miserable. I've been involved in that foolishness myself (BC . . . before Carole). It's silly.

You learn a lot about other people and you learn a lot about yourself when dating. Some of it is good. Some if it isn't quite so good. That's just part of life. Tennyson said, "'Tis better to have loved and lost than never to have loved at all."[7] I think that's true. But what Elvis Presley sang in All Shook Up[8] is better.

Please don't ask me what's on my mind
I'm a little mixed up but I'm feeling fine
When I'm near TJC that I love best
My heart beats so it scares me to death

Go out (or whatever it is you do these days). Have a nice time. And be home by midnight (just kidding).

Things to Think About:

✓ How do you meet people? Where do you meet them?

✓ Does dating make you nervous or are you comfortable meeting new people?

✓ Would you date someone you know you would never marry?

✓ Is it okay to say yes to a date just because you want to go to dinner or have good seats at a concert or game?

S-E-X

That is why a man leaves his father and mother and is
united to his wife, and they become one flesh.
GENESIS 2:24

Boys and girls in America have such a sad time together;
sophistication demands that they submit to sex immediately
without proper preliminary talk. Not courting talk—real straight
talk about souls, for life is holy and every moment is precious.
JACK KEROUAC

People have been having sex since the mid-1700's. Okay, it's really been longer than that—much longer. Just read the Bible. The world is created in Genesis chapter one. Adam and Eve meet in chapter two. They realize they are naked in chapter three. And by chapter four they have two kids. Let that be a lesson to you.

Sex, and lots if it, is in the Bible. In fact, people were begetting all over the place. Sex is not some new threat to civilization, although to hear some people tell it you would think it is. Sex is not dirty and it is not shameful. It is a wonderful thing. Sex is a gift from God. But always remember it is a gift that brings with it a tremendous responsibility.

The Bible says sex should be experienced within marriage, and I think there is much to be learned from those passages. That's not to say I'm giving the Bible my stamp of approval. Ultimately, my opinion doesn't matter at all. God is God and I am not. The point I'm trying to make is that what God tells us makes sense and should be respected. It's not like God sits up in heaven, far removed from us, making up arbitrary rules. God guides us out of love for us. God wants what is best for us and is eager to teach us—if only we will listen. The Bible is filled with practical wisdom that will help us, and that is certainly the case with sex.

Let's pause here for a quick side note: Even though it's true the Bible offers practical information, the Bible is much more than a handy "Tips for Good Living" manual. The Holy Bible is primary to our faith, sufficient in all things, revealing the Word of God so far as it is necessary to our salvation. Now back to our regularly scheduled program . . .

Sex is an expression of love. It is a wonderfully intimate sharing of self. It is the joining of two people that may lead to three. Sex is special and should never be cheapened. There is nothing casual about it.

The trouble is, many (or maybe most) of the messages our culture sends about sex are the opposite of that standard. Sex sells and sex entertains. Just look at television, for example (and by no means is it just television, it's everywhere): Everybody's doing it. Anytime. Anyplace. With anybody. And if you're not, there must be something wrong with you. Abstinence is considered a personality flaw. Does culture reflect media? Sure it does. But media also reflect a culture that already exists. Like I said, sex isn't new. And neither is promiscuity.

The Bible does not shy away from sex. Some of the stories are about the expression of love, and there are plenty of the other kind, too. If you read those stories, one thing you'll notice is that bad decisions often lead to unpleasant consequences. The same is true today. So does that mean the girl gets pregnant the first time? No. Quite often that's not what happens at all. Will you go blind? I doubt it (although I find it interesting when teen-agers wear glasses). Will you be struck dead? Probably not. Will fire rain down from Heaven? Clearly not . . . we still have Las Vegas. Will other terrible things happen? Maybe. Maybe not.

However, something will happen. You can count on it. It may be severe or it may be subtle, but there will be something. The thing to remember is you have the freedom to choose, and all choices result in consequences. Bad choices, bad consequences. Good choices, good consequences.

When the Bible talks about sex, the ultimate point is not the physical act. It's the emotional act. It's not a matter of the body. It's a matter of the heart and soul. It's about love or the lack of it. Do they love each other? Do they respect each other? Are they honoring each other? You see, it's not about sex (and always remember that sex and love are not the same thing). It's about love, respect, and honor. What the Bible teaches is that when you lose respect and honor for yourself and for other people, and when you act out of selfish interests rather than acting out of love, bad things start to happen.

 When you lose respect and honor for yourself and for other people, and when you act out of selfish interests rather than acting out of love, bad things start to happen.

That, however, is easier said than done. The challenge you and everyone your age have had for some time now is that you're going through life as a walking hormone. That's not a bad thing. In fact, it's all very natural. Your body has changed from child to adult and a strong sex drive is part of the package. To make matters even more challenging, you now have more freedom than you've ever had in your life. Not only are you away from home every night, you'll also have your own swinging party pad (I know that's very 1970s of me, but I just couldn't help myself) and a world full of alluring people. You'll find that although your mind and heart may be telling you to wait, your body will be telling you to be fruitful and multiply.

I could just say don't have sex . . . DON'T HAVE SEX . . . okay, there it is . . . I said it. But I understand it's not that simple because no one can make this decision for you. It's a decision only you can make. So here's what I suggest: Ask yourself (better yet, ask each other) whether you are both acting out of love or acting out of lust. Is your relationship respectful and honorable? Have you thought it through and considered the short-term and long-term consequences (both bad and good) or are you acting out of passion? Who's doing the thinking? Are you thinking? Will you want to take it back in the morning? You can't.

As I said before, sex is a great gift that comes with tremendous responsibility. It's not just about you. It's about the other person, too. And it's about every other person you have a relationship with past, present, and future. It's also about the person you'll marry, even if you haven't met yet. The actions you take will impact the rest of your life. And sometimes they change your life, and other lives, forever.

Things to Think About:

✓ Why do you think we find it so awkward to discuss sex when it's all around us in popular culture? What messages do you see in popular culture?

✓ In what ways are men and women different when it comes to sex? Do you agree that men tend to be physically involved while women tend to be emotionally involved?

✓ Do you get the feeling "everybody's doing it" even though few people in church and faith groups are willing to admit it and talk about it?

MARRIAGE

But Ruth replied, 'Don't urge me to leave you or to turn back
from you. Where you go I will go, and where you stay
I will stay. Your people will be my people and your God my God.
Where you die I will die, and there I will be buried.
May the LORD deal with me, be it ever so severely, if anything
but death separates you and me.'

RUTH 1:16

People always fall in love with the most perfect aspects of each
other's personalities. Who wouldn't? Anybody can love the most
wonderful parts of another person. But that's not the clever trick.
The really clever trick is this: Can you accept the flaws? Can you
look at your partner's faults honestly and say, 'I can work around
that. I can make something out of it.'? Because the good stuff is
always going to be there, and it's always going to be pretty and
sparkly, but the crap underneath can ruin you.

ELIZABETH GILBERT

used to wonder how I would know when I was ready to get married. It was a scary thought. How do I choose a woman to spend the rest of my life with? There are millions of them. And what if the person I like doesn't like me? She had to choose me, too, and that was a really scary thought. I was nervous just thinking about asking someone out for a date. What do we talk about? What do we do? And if I can't figure that out for one date, what's it going to be like if we're married? Isn't marriage just a date that never ends? And I've been on a couple of dates I thought would never end, but that's another story.

Well, don't worry. You'll know. Looking back on it all, it's not as bad as it seemed at the time. Of course, that doesn't make it any easier when you're going through it.

I can't say just how it will be for you, and I don't know how it goes for other people, but for me an amazing thing happened. When I met my lovely wife-to-be, Carole, I knew she was the one for me. Was it love at first sight? I'm not sure. But if not, it was pretty darn close. I wasn't planning to get married at that time in my life. It certainly wasn't a goal I had set. I never felt I had to be married by a certain age. Suddenly, there she was, and I just knew I would rather be with her than anyone else in the whole world. That's still true today. Not only do I love Carole, I like her, too. She's fun to pal around with. We watch old movies, go camping, and go out to dinner. Sometimes I go shopping with her and she goes to baseball games with me (that's true sacrifice for both of us).

Carole is my best friend—and that's the point. I was first attracted to her because I thought she would be fun to hang out with (and she was really cute . . . still is). It was that simple. We just kind of jumped in to see what would happen. If it worked, it worked, and if it didn't, it didn't. Fortunately for me, it worked.

Don't go looking for the perfect spouse. There is no such thing . . . and Carole will be quick to agree. Find a friend. Find your best friend. That's when you'll know you're on to something.

I think some people run into the problem of falling in lust rather than falling in love. They want a certain look or a certain style. They want one of the beautiful people. They are attracted physically, but there is nothing beyond the passion. That won't last. Now, don't misunderstand . . . I love Carole passionately (and it probably gives you the willies for me to say that out loud), but there must be depth to a relationship, too. That's what sustains it. A depth made of love, friendship, and compassion. And a little passion sure doesn't hurt.

And once you're married . . . well, that's when the work really begins. When you're mad (and you will be) or when something is bothering you (and it will), don't expect the other person to know. Talk about it. Work through it. But always remember working through something and fixing it are not the same thing. Don't dare go into marriage recognizing problems but thinking, "I'll fix that after we're married." No you won't. You won't "fix" anything, but you sure will create a lot of resentment.

✓ We have agreed divorce is not an option and that sure changes how we approach things because there's no getting out. So we know we have to work it out and we know we have to work through it.

Be respectful in all things. Be respectful to each other and about each other. Never say anything about your spouse you wouldn't say to your spouse. Better yet, never say anything at all that does not honor or compliment your spouse in some way. Trust each other and be trustworthy.

Also, be committed to each other. Carole and I have agreed divorce is not an option, and that sure changes how we approach things because we know there's no getting out. So we know we have to talk it out and we know we have to work through it. Please understand, when I say divorce is not an option, I'm writing about the commitment Carole and I have made to each other. I realize there are abusive marriages and in no way do I intend to imply that abuse should be condoned. Abuse is absolutely unacceptable, be it physical, mental, emotional, or verbal. Abuse should never be tolerated.

So share small kindnesses. Enjoy each other's company. Never take each other for granted. Keep dating . . . keep winning each other's hearts. Also understand you're separate people, so you'll need a little "me" time, too. That's a good thing . . . as long as it's not all about "me."

Marriage is wonderful. I highly recommend it. But then again, I did marry above myself.

Things to Think About:

✓ How will you know when you're ready to get married?

✓ In what ways is friendship important to a marriage?

✓ What impact does the idea of "divorce is not an option" have on a relationship? Are there exceptions?

✓ Why should you keep dating after you're married? How do you do that?

THE LITTLE THINGS

My dear brothers and sisters, take note of this:
Everyone should be quick to listen, slow to speak and slow
to become angry, because human anger does not
produce the righteous life that God desires.
JAMES 1:19-20

Do not forget that the value and interest of life is
not so much to do conspicuous things . . . as to do ordinary things
with the perception of their enormous value.
PIERRE TEILHARD DE CHARDIN

The first year of marriage is always a challenge. Some people say it's the toughest year of all. Does that surprise you? How could it be tough? Dating was great. The engagement was a whirlwind of excitement. The wedding was perfect. You're in love. You're in lust. And now you are together always and forever. That's the problem. You will both have so much to learn about each other. You will still have to figure each other out. You may think that happens during dating and engagement, and to a certain degree it does, but the reality is you just don't know someone until you live with them. You just don't know someone (or yourself) until you realize you both live in the same place and there is nowhere to hide and there is no escape.

One of the most important thoughts to keep in mind during your first year together (and every year after for that matter) is that it's not the big things that matter most—it's the little things. The big things do matter, of course, but because they are big you are forced to deal with them. In other words, a big problem is like an elephant in the room. You see him and you get him out of there (or you're going to have a big mess).

 You just don't know someone (or yourself) until you realize you both live in the same place and there is nowhere to hide and there is no escape.

Little problems are more like termites. They hide under the surface, so you don't know there is a problem until the house comes crashing down.

The point is this: Pay attention. Understand what's important to you (even the little things) and make sure you know what is important to your spouse (especially the little things). Do those things that are uplifting and avoid everything that is annoying. Communicate. You're in it together, so you're going to have to work it out. You're going to have to talk it out. And (maybe most important of all) you're going to have to listen it out.

One more thing: When (and notice I said when) you and your sweetie are having an argument, what you think you're discussing is not really what the argument is about at all. You're really dealing with those little things that have built up over time. It was set off by the one termite that went too far.

On a related note, I would encourage you to read *The Five Love Languages* by Gary Chapman.[9] It is simply brilliant and one of the best relationship books I have ever read. It's all about the little things.

Things to Think About:

✓ Why is it easy to miss the little things? Why are they so important?

✓ Why is it that you don't really know someone until you live with them?

✓ How do you deal with these issues before they build up? How do you work it out?

JUST SAY THANK YOU

Therefore encourage one another and build each other up,
just as in fact you are doing.
I THESSALONIANS 5:11

I feel a very unusual sensation—if it is not indigestion,
I think it must be gratitude.
BENJAMIN DISRAELI

One of the realities of marriage is there will be times you will drive each other nuts. You'll ask yourself, "What was I thinking when I married this crazy person?" And, believe me, your spouse will be thinking that . . . and more . . . about you. It's just one of those marriage things. If you spend that much time with someone, it's inevitable you'll get on each other's nerves.

One way to avoid that problem is common courtesy. Be kind to each other—even though that is much easier said than done.

Another way to avoid getting on each other's nerves is not getting worked up over things that really don't matter. Pick your battles (and that's not to say you're at war with each other . . . although some couples sure seem to be). Don't be bothered by unimportant things. If you have to discuss/fuss/fight, make sure the problem is worth the effort. Make sure it's important. Important may be big and important may be small (it's the thousands of little things, after all), but I think you'll find many of those "things" don't matter quite as much when you focus on the big picture.

For example, I was talking with a couple-to-be once about communication in marriage. The husband is a fine man and a dear friend. He works hard at the office and he works hard at home (both inside and out). He's intelligent, kind, and caring, but he's also (by his own admission) a bit of a perfectionist. During one of our pre-marriage counseling sessions, he recognized the importance of open, honest communication, so he asked a very good and very sincere question. And I'll give him credit . . . he had the courage to ask that question with his fiancé sitting right next to him on the couch. "Well," he said. "What if she's cooking something and it's not very good? What if I know how to do it better? What should I say?" My reply . . . "Just say thank you."

✓ Don't criticize. Don't offer suggestions for improvement. The cool thing is your spouse is doing something nice for you. Just say thank you. Then do something nice for your spouse.

So the moral of the story is this: Don't criticize. Don't offer suggestions for improvement. The cool thing is your spouse is doing something nice for you. Just say thank you. Then do something nice for your spouse.

One more thing: Husbands, help out without being asked. And when she wants to talk about a problem she's having, shut up and listen. Don't try to fix it. Wives, don't offer advice (or criticism) on a project your husband is working on when you've not been specifically asked for help. And you probably won't be.[10]

126

Things to Think About:

✓ What's the difference between a small issue and a big issue? What matters most in marriage? What are the most important things?

✓ Do you have to work at saying thank you or is it natural for you?

✓ Do you think men and women tend to approach giving and receiving advice differently?

✓ How do you give advice? How do you receive it?

60/40

Love is patient, love is kind. It does not envy,
it does not boast, it is not proud. It does not dishonor others,
it is not self-seeking, it is not easily angered, it keeps no
record of wrongs. Love does not delight in evil but rejoices
with the truth. It always protects, always trusts,
always hopes, always perseveres. Love never fails.

I CORINTHIANS 13:4-8

People who love each other need to have something they can do
for each other, and it will need to be something necessary,
not something frivolous. You can't carry out a relationship on the
basis of Christmas and anniversary and birthday presents.
It won't work. You have to be doing something that you need help
with, and your wife has to be doing something she needs
help with. You do needful, useful things for each other, and that
seems to me to be the way union is made.

WENDELL BERRY

Much is said these days about equality and how marriage should be a partnership where the husband and wife split everything down the middle—50/50. I think that's a bad idea. The problem with a 50/50 split is that each side tends to keep count so they can stop at fifty percent. Or, more likely, to make sure the other person is not getting away with something by doing less than half of the work.

I think marriages should be split 60/40 . . . with each side dedicated to doing sixty percent. Each person expects to do a little more

128

than the other—to serve the other. So rather than each one keeping score, each one should give extra effort out of love.

✓ The problem with a 50/50 split is that each side tends to keep count so they can stop at fifty percent. Or, more likely, to make sure the other person is not getting away with something by doing less than half of the work.

It's looking for ways to help each other and support each other. It's looking for ways to help with the heavy lifting. And maybe it's looking for ways to help with the light lifting, too. It comes down to the simple things . . . those repetitive chores that can be so aggravating.

I think most couples tend to divide those things up. It may be somewhat formal, sort of like picking teams. Or it may be more informal in that one person just takes on certain things along the way.

However you divide up responsibilities in your marriage, try to help out and do some of those small jobs the other person usually does. Don't leave it for them. Do it yourself. (I made up the bed this morning—bonus points for me). Drive the kids, put gas in the car (those two often go together), take out the trash, or fold the clothes (I hate that one). Cook supper and clean up.

This all sounds pretty simple, but it's actually harder than you might think. We all have good days and not so good days. Everyone falls off to forty percent every now and then. But as long as the other person is giving sixty percent on those off days, you still have a one hundred percent marriage. And just think how nice it will be when you're both clicking along at sixty.

I'm going to empty the dishwasher now.

Things to Think About:

✓ How have you and your spouse (or roommate) divided up the chores?

✓ What are some of the "heavy lifting" type responsibilities you can help out with? What about on the "light lifting" side?

✓ How can we move from keeping score to being eager to do a little more?

LOW EXPECTATIONS

Do not judge, and you will not be judged. Do not condemn,
and you will not be condemned. Forgive, and you will be forgiven.
Give, and it will be given to you. A good measure, pressed down,
shaken together and running over, will be poured into your lap.
For with the measure you use, it will be measured to you.
LUKE 6:37-38

When you stop expecting people to be perfect,
you can like them for who they are.
DONALD MILLER

My lovely wife, Carole, often says the reason she's happy being married to me is because she has low expectations. Fortunately for me, she says it with a smile. It's pretty funny and it's also very insightful. Carole and I do have low expectations . . . and high standards. We don't expect everything to be perfect because if you do expect perfection, you'll never be content. Life just doesn't work that way. Never has. Never will. People are people so things go wrong.

That's especially true in relationships. Real-life marriage is not like an old black-and-white romantic movie and Carole and I are not Deborah Kerr and Cary Grant in *An Affair to Remember*. Come to think of it, you may have never heard of that one. Think Meg Ryan and Tom Hanks in *Sleepless in Seattle*. Well, that one may be a little old, too. How about Kate Winslet and Leonardo DiCaprio in *Titanic*? Mandy Moore and Shane West in *A Walk to Remember*? The point is marriage has its ups and downs and plateaus. There are good days, bad days, and mediocre days. You'll have joys, issues, and aggravations (there are a lot of aggravations, just ask Carole). Enjoy the good times and the sweet moments. Don't obsess over the shortcomings. In fact, the shortcomings can be a blessing because within those faults is an opportunity for grace. Be merciful and forgiving. Love each other.

 The shortcomings can be a blessing because within those faults is an opportunity for grace.

And now that I have said that, let me say this . . . establish high standards. Determine to be the best you can be. Love and support your family so they can always be their best.

Perhaps that sounds like a contradiction but it's not. It's all a matter of proportion. It's about understanding that life is good even though it's not perfect. Have reasonable expectations but never settle. Have high standards but know people can be messy. Love your family for who they are and never be disappointed in who they are not.

Things to Think About:

✓ What's the difference between low expectations and high standards?

✓ When are there opportunities for grace in relationships?

✓ People are people so things go wrong . . . why is that?

COULDN'T DO ANY BETTER

Again, the kingdom of heaven is like a merchant looking
for fine pearls. When he found one of great value, he went away
and sold everything he had and bought it.

MATTHEW 13:45-46

Be calm, only by a calm consideration of our existence can
we achieve our purpose to live together - Be calm - love me -
today - yesterday - what tearful longings for you . . . my life
- my all . . . Oh continue to love me - never misjudge the most
faithful heart of your beloved. Ever thine . . . ever mine . . . ever ours.

LUDWIG VAN BEETHOVEN TO HIS IMMORTAL BELOVED

When my lovely wife, Carole, says she married me because she had low expectations, I like to say I married her because I couldn't do any better. I say that to be funny, but I really do mean it—at the deeper level of appreciating who and what I have.

I've never been one to believe there is only one person in this world for me. I guess I could have found someone else and been equally happy. Maybe. However, I know those "some ones" are extremely rare and absolutely no one could be more wonderful than the one I got (and who got me). Carole is as good as it gets, so I couldn't have done any better.

There's an old saying that the grass is always greener on the other side of the fence. That's just another way of saying what we don't have is more appealing than what we do have. Perhaps the grass does look greener, but it's really not . . . it's just different grass. And trading one thing for another rarely brings the satisfaction we think it will . . . it just brings a new set of problems.

✓ There's an old saying that the grass is always greener on the other side of the fence. That's just another way of saying what we don't have is more appealing than what we do have. Perhaps the grass does look greener, but it's really not . . . it's just different grass.

Our culture is fascinated with the best, the biggest, the new and improved. There is always a new model, the latest feature, the thing you gotta have. Don't fall into that trap. Don't believe it. It's a lie.

Find that special someone. It may take a while, but that's okay. It's worth it. There is no deadline. Marriage is not a race or a contest. And when you do find that special someone—when you find each other—commit to each other. Uplift each other. Love each other. You can't do any better. It's the best there is.

Things to Think About:

✓ What is it about the things we don't have that may make them more appealing than what we do have?

✓ Have you ever had to have the "new thing" only to find out it wasn't what you thought it would be once you got it? Could it be the excitement is in the chase?

✓ What does it mean to commit to another person, forsaking all others?

(IT'S A) FAMILY TRADITION

And let us consider how we may spur one another on toward
love and good deeds, not giving up meeting together, as some are
in the habit of doing, but encouraging one another—and all
the more as you see the Day approaching.
HEBREWS 10:24-25

'Home is the place where, when you have to go there,
They have to take you in.'
'I should have called it
Something you somehow haven't to deserve.'
ROBERT FROST (FROM THE DEATH OF THE HIRED MAN)[11]

Many things go into the making of a family . . . mothers, fathers, children, brothers, sisters, grandparents, aunts, uncles, and cousins. Plus, there are those people we may not be officially related to that we still consider family. The sad thing is, it's actually possible to be related to people in that "official" way and still not be true family.

Family is about love and commitment, and many other things as well. Family is where we are at home and with whom we are at home. You know the old saying, "Home is where the heart is." Love is there. I like that. Robert Frost wrote, "Home is the place where, when you have to go there, they have to take you in." Commitment is there. I like that, too.

Another important part of family is shared experiences. It's all of those things we do together. It's living our lives with each other. It's

137

sharing joys, sorrows, victories, defeats. Often times, it's just hanging out together. Our traditions and all of those moments we share make us who we are as a family.

 We did not adopt these traditions because they were inherently special. They became special because our family adopted them.

In our family, we have our own set of traditions: pizza & movie night, car trips (we once drove cross-country to the Grand Canyon and back . . . man-oh-man America is a big place), Christmas morning pancakes, and a few others, too. We did not adopt these traditions because they were inherently special. They became special because our family adopted them.

When your family comes along, you may continue some of your family's traditions, but be sure to create traditions of your own. They don't have to be elaborate. They sure don't have to be expensive. I think it's the simple things that are the best. The main thing is it's family and you make a point of spending time together.

Things to Think About:

✓ What are you favorite family traditions? What makes them special?

✓ How can you create traditions with your extended family? Do you and your friends have established traditions?

✓ What traditions would you like to create for your family and friends?

(OUR) FAMILY VALUES

But be very careful to keep the commandment and the law that
Moses the servant of the LORD gave you: to love the LORD your God,
to walk in obedience to him, to keep his commands, to hold fast to
him and to serve him with all your heart and with all your soul.

JOSHUA 22:5

In the family, happiness is in the ratio in which each is
serving the others, seeking one another's good,
and bearing one another's burdens.

HENRY WARD BEECHER

Part of being a family is knowing who you are. It's knowing what you believe in, what you stand for, and how you choose to live. In our family we've tried to recognize the important things in life and do our best to focus on what matters most. Please understand, we don't always get it right. Sometimes, in fact, we absolutely blow it, but we do try. And it seems we learn something new every day, so I hope we're getting better as we go along.

These values are at the core of who we are as a family. This is who we are when it's just us. And it's who we should be whenever we leave the house or when other people come to visit us. We should be the same people and have the same values if we're alone as a family or with others, if we're inside our house or out.

You and your spouse will have to establish values for your family. Don't leave it to chance, it's too important for that. Be intentional about who you want to be as a family because, intentional or not, it's going to happen.

Just in case you wanted to know, here are the values we intend for our family:

Love (of God, our neighbors, and ourselves)

Faith & Worship

Good Work

Honesty

Respect

Knowledge & Education

Art & Music

Healthy Living

Fun & Fellowship

A list of words on paper probably doesn't mean much. It's better to think of these things in more practical ways. Others can see our values in how we live (and that's much more important than what we say). We worship, pray, and study. We honor God, other people, and each other in the way we go about our lives. We understand that it's not about us. We're not the center of the universe.

We choose work we believe in and that makes a difference in some small way. We sit down for dinner together most every night. We love each other no matter what. We tell the truth. We treat each other—and other people—the way we want to be treated. We read good books. We listen to music and play a little music, too. We draw and paint (actually, my wonderful son, Harry, is the artist, not me). We eat good food (and some stuff that's just good for the soul). We have fun together. We go outside and play (play sounds much more fun than exercise). We are courteous to each other and show respect for each other (most of the time). And when we do get tired and aggravated and start to snap at each other, we know we're out of line and we apologize (I need to be much better about this one). It's all about the tone we set.

Be intentional about creating positive moments with your family.

The reality of family life is that you'll frustrate and irritate each other from time to time. Since you know the negatives are inevitable, make a point of creating happy times to outnumber the not so happy. That way, when those negatives do arise, they will be a small part of a much larger warm environment.

 We should be the same people and have the same values if we're alone as a family or with others, if we're inside our house or out.

Likewise, be intentional also about creating a standard of encouragement and support for your family, especially your children. It will be necessary to correct your kids along the way. They are young, they are learning, and they need your guidance. Yes, you will have to "get after" them sometimes, but it's a matter of proportion. Make sure your good words far exceed—by a wide margin—the bad. And remember, too, correction done in love is ultimately positive.

The idea of family values is not terribly complicated and there's really nothing unique about our values. It all comes down to loving each other. It all comes down to knowing this is who we are and this is what we do. And when we mess up (which we often do) we don't give up.

Things to Think About:

✓ What family values did you have growing up? What values do you want for your future family?

✓ Why is it important to have the same values all of the time, no matter where you are or who you're with?

✓ Why should we be intentional about establishing family values?

JUST SHOW UP

Finally, brothers and sisters, whatever is true, whatever is noble,
whatever is right, whatever is pure, whatever is lovely,
whatever is admirable—if anything is excellent or
praiseworthy—think about such things.
PHILIPPIANS 4:8

God, whether I get anything else done today, I want to make sure
that I spend time loving you and loving other people—because
that's what life is all about. I don't want to waste this day.
PETER J. GOMES

think half the battle in life is just showing up. It's true for school,
it's true for work, and it's certainly true for family. I've known a lot
of really smart people who did poorly in school or work just because
they didn't show up. I've known some people who claim to love
their families, but the families fell apart because they didn't show up.

There are actually two parts to this idea of showing up. One is pretty
obvious . . . you have to be there physically. Be in class. Be at work. Be at
home . . . or wherever your children are as they play ball, perform in plays,
or do whatever it is they do. How you spend your time is a true indication
of what you value most, and the most valuable thing you can provide for
your family is *you*.

The other part to showing up is actually more important . . . it's
showing up with all you have. It's possible to be in one place physically but be in another world mentally and emotionally. We can spend

144

hours in the same space with someone but have absolutely no connection with that person. So the key is to focus on what's most important and not be distracted by the noisy things . . . like cell phones . . . social media . . . even that noise in our heads as we worry about all of those things we worry about.

✓ It's possible to be in one place physically but be in another world mentally and emotionally. We can spend hours in the same space with someone but have absolutely no connection with them.

Whatever it is you're doing, do that thing with all you have. Be fully present. When you're in class, be fully in class. When you're at work, be fully at work. And most important of all, when you're with your family, be fully with your family.

Things to Think About:

✓ What's the difference in being physically present and emotionally present?

✓ What do you find to be most distracting for you? How do you deal with it?

✓ How do you say "no" to distractions and "yes" to the more important things?

THIS TOO SHALL PASS

What do workers gain from their toil? I have seen the burden God
has laid on the human race. He has made everything beautiful in
its time. He has also set eternity in the human heart; yet no one
can fathom what God has done from beginning to end.
ECCLESIASTES 3:9-11

When things are bad, remember: It won't always be this way.
Take one day at a time. When things are good, remember: It won't
always be this way. Enjoy every great moment.
DOE ZANTAMATA

Back when my wonderful son, Harry, was a little fellow and still
sleeping in a crib, he would catch a cold and get all stopped
up. He slept with a pacifier so that meant he couldn't breathe.
His nose was stopped up and he had a stopper in his mouth.
That's a bad combination.

One night, there was nothing my lovely wife, Carole, and I could
do that would get him back to sleep. We had tried everything. It was
about two or three in the morning and we were tired, sleepy, and at
our wit's end.

Then we had an idea. Harry always fell asleep in the car, so we
thought we would give it a try. At that point anything was worth a try.
We put him in the car cradle and off we went. It was the middle of the
night and we were driving around town in our pajamas. That may sound
crazy but it worked! He was asleep in about fifteen minutes. We drove

back to the house and gently took him out of the car. Then we put the car cradle down in the crib and he slept through the rest of the night . . . what little was left.

 Whatever it is, it too shall pass. Oddly enough, we may even miss some of those tough times.

And then there were the earaches. I remember one of the many late nights with Harry thinking, "I'm not going to sleep for the next twenty-one years." I knew that wasn't true, of course, but it sure felt like it at the time. What I also remember thinking at the time was, "This too shall pass." And it did.

There will be times in life you'll have to endure. Some of them are relatively simple . . . like a colicky child or a tough stretch at work. Others are much more troubling . . . like serious illness or deep financial problems. Whatever it is, it too shall pass.

Oddly enough, we may even miss some of those tough times. Life is lived there. Love is experienced there. As strange as it may seem, a part of me misses being up with Harry in the middle of the night. He was small and needed me. I was there for him when it counted. I think back on that now those times have passed.[12]

Things to Think About:

✓ How were things for your parents when you were a child? If you ask, they may have some entertaining stories to tell. And then ask your grandparents what things were like for them.

✓ Have you ever stayed up all night with someone you care about? What made the sacrifice of sleep worth it?

✓ Is there something in your life now you hope will soon pass? Is there something you hope will never end?

WHO YOUR FRIENDS ARE(N'T)

A friend loves at all times, and a brother is
born for a time of adversity.
PROVERBS 17:17

It is one of the blessings of old friends
that you can afford to be stupid with them.
RALPH WALDO EMERSON

think you can divide friends into two basic categories: circumstantial friends and soul friends. The problem is you can't always tell the difference right away.

Circumstantial friends are those people you're connected to because of circumstances you share. You work together. Maybe you go to church together. It may be that you're in some group or civic organization.

Soul friends are those people you connect with in a special way. You're not friends merely because of circumstances, you're friends because you have a genuine bond with each other that often transcends circumstances.

Let me say there is nothing wrong at all with circumstantial friends. Friendships come in all shapes and sizes and every relationship is different. Some are deep and strong, lasting for many years. Others are more casual (but still good), lasting a short time. But no matter what type of friendship it is, you'll have to give it time and effort.

Friendships have to be nurtured. That's why circumstantial friendships change once the circumstances change. The friendship is no longer convenient or easy, so it tends to fade away. That's not to say you have a falling out, it means only that you move on in new directions.

The fact of the matter is most friendships have life spans. They just won't last a lifetime, although it's a rare and wonderful thing when they do. It's quite natural for friendships to dissolve (usually without any drama at all) and for your lives to move on. Sometimes we cross paths again somewhere down the road and the friendship is rekindled. That's always a cool thing when it happens.

✓ Friendships come in all shapes and sizes and every relationship is different. Some are deep and strong lasting for many years. Others are more casual (but still good) lasting a short time.

What I'm really getting at is this: How do you know the difference between a circumstantial friend and a soul friend? I think you find out who your true friends are . . . who your soul friends are . . . when times get tough. You find out who your friends are . . . and who they aren't . . . when you face a crisis of some sort.

A fact of life is that you will face hard times along the way. It may be something that happens to you, it may be something you bring on yourself. Nevertheless, you will face a few hard times in life.

Your soul friends are those friends who stand with you in the tough times. They're not friends just because things are going well. They're not friends just because things are convenient or beneficial for them (which really isn't friendship at all). They are not friends merely because of favorable circumstances. They're friends because they love you and care for you because of who you are as a person. They are the people who will stand beside you when bad things happen. They are also the people who will call you out when they see you're making bad decisions.

When times get tough you'll find out who your friends are and you'll find out who your friends aren't. And you'll be surprised. There will be people you thought you could count on who will suddenly turn invisible. There will be others who will astound you with their grace. And, of course, there will be those people you always knew you could count on and there they are with a kind word or a helping hand. In fact, it may be there is nothing to say or nothing that can be done, but they are there for you . . . and just being there is often the best thing.

Things to Think About:

✓ Are there people you are fond of who are circumstantial friends? Do you think it will ever move to soul friends?

✓ Are there circumstantial friends you miss because your lives have moved in different directions? Are there soul friends you miss? What happened? Can the friendship be restored?

✓ Who are your soul friends? What is it about them (and you) that brings the friendship to that level?

✓ Have you ever had a friend surprise you with their grace? How might you surprise someone with your grace?

FAITH

I BELIEVE

We have come to believe and to know
that you are the Holy One of God.
JOHN 6:69

When we get our spiritual house in order, we'll be dead. This goes
on: you arrive at enough certainty to be able to make your way,
but it is making it in darkness. Don't expect faith to clear things
up for you. It is trust, not certainty.
FLANNERY O'CONNOR

certainly don't have all of the answers to the big questions of faith.
I haven't even thought of all the questions yet . . . and never will.
How could I? How could any of us?

It's tempting to want to explain God and to put God in a pretty
little box with a bow on top, but to do so would mean we're bigger
than God, that we've put our arms around God the way we do a neatly
wrapped present. That's impossible.

God is bigger than we are. Infinitely bigger. It's not for us to explain
God, but it is for us to worship, to ponder, and to trust. As Kirby Godsey[13] says, "The beginning of faith is learning that God's arms are
around us."[14]

These thoughts on faith are not intended to be lessons or sermons
(please forgive me if I come across as teachy and preachy; it's an occu-
pational hazard) but rather conversations, conversations that serve as
building blocks of faith. As you continue reading, please take time to

ponder and pray. Engage yourself and other people. Exchange ideas and test them with Scripture complemented by the experience, reason, and tradition of fellow believers. Arrive at your own conclusions. Learn and grow always.

 God is bigger than we are. Infinitely bigger. It's not for us to explain God, but it is for us to worship, to ponder, and to trust.

Ultimately, we must all make our faith our own. We must move beyond what we have been taught to what we experience. Faith is not merely learning the "right" answers to the "right" questions. Honest faith is lived here and now in the reality of life and death, love and scorn, joy and pain, confidence and doubt.

I will begin the discussion with my confession of who I am and where I stand in this moment as God continues the work of grace in me.

I believe in the beginning God and forever God.

I believe in the grace of God through the love of Jesus Christ.

I believe that by grace I am saved through faith, yet without works, my faith is dead.

I believe God is love.

I believe I should love the Lord my God with all my heart and soul and mind and strength.

And I believe I should love my neighbor as myself.

One more thing: I have come to understand that "I don't know" is an acceptable answer. It doesn't mean I've given up, it just means I don't know.

Things to Think About:

✓ What do you believe? Does it change over time? Should it?

✓ What is the difference between faith as an answer to a question and faith as a way of life?

✓ Have you ever considered writing out a statement of faith . . . the foundation of what you believe?

✓ Do you agree or disagree with Flannery O'Connor that our faith is more trust than certainty?

✓ What's the difference between "I don't know" and giving up?

REMEMBER WHO YOU ARE

So do not throw away your confidence; it will be richly rewarded.
You need to persevere so that when you have done the will of God,
you will receive what he has promised.

HEBREWS 10:35-36

In a world of fugitives, the person taking the opposite direction
will appear to be running away.

T. S. ELIOT

Dietrich Bonheoffer said, "To be simple is to fix one's eye solely on the simple truth of God at a time when all concepts are being confused, distorted and turned upside down."[15] That is a wise observation which especially holds true in our age of epistemological indeterminacy. EI is just a fancy (and rather pretentious on my part) way of saying there is more to know than we can possibly know. Think of it as drinking water from a fire hose, but rather than drowning in water, we're drowning in information. We can be so overwhelmed by competing facts, theories, and opinions we don't know where to start or where to stop. How do we find simple truth in an on-rushing stream?

I find my focus is sharpened by praying, studying, reading the Bible, and reading what wise people have to say. These things help me know the simple truth of God and remind me of what is ultimately important. I've noticed that it's when I forget what matters most that things start going wrong. It's a sure sign I've forgotten what I need to remember.

As difficult as that remembering can be for me, I'm sure it can be even more difficult for you. I've been around long enough that I've had time to figure some things out. Since you're just now setting out on your own, virtually everything is new to you. How can you *remember* who you are when you don't even *know* who you are yet? That's not a bad thing and I certainly don't mean it in a condescending way, it's just a fact of life. I'm still learning every day (at least I hope I am . . . I sure need to be).

 The main thing to remember as you begin to drink from the fire hose is this simple truth: God loves you.

The main thing to remember as you drink from the fire hose is this simple truth: God loves you. You'll come across people who don't believe that about themselves. They won't believe it about you and they won't believe it about anybody. Don't listen to them. Remember who you are. You are a child of God.

Things to Think About:

✓ Are there times you've felt like you're drinking from a fire hose?

✓ How do you sort through all the information?

✓ What are the simple truths you hold on to?

✓ How do you grow in knowledge and wisdom while honoring your core values?

✓ What are your core values? Do they change? Should they change?

IN THE IMAGE OF GOD

And so we know and rely on the love God has for us. God is love.
Whoever lives in love lives in God, and God in them.
I JOHN 4:16

The deepest desire of our hearts is for union with God.
God created us for union with himself.
This is the original purpose of our lives.
BRENNAN MANNING

bet if you asked a Vacation Bible School class to draw a picture of God, many—boys and girls both—would draw a man with a gray beard sitting on a golden throne. We like to see God as one of us. We see God bigger, stronger, and more powerful than we are but otherwise much like ourselves. We have made God in our image. We do it with Jesus, too. Take a look at all the blue-eyed, sharp nosed Jesus pictures you find in Sunday school classrooms. "I dream of Jesus with the light brown hair." That's just not what a middle-eastern Jew looked like.

While Jesus-the-Son did have a human body, God-the-Father is not red or yellow, black or white, and God is not male or female in the sense we think about those things. Now, I know the Bible frequently describes God as "he" and "father," but we should keep in mind the Bible also uses feminine imagery to help us understand the true nature of God (for example, Isaiah 66:12 and Matthew 23:37).

You'll notice I sometimes refer to God as "he." That's the language I grew up with, so I'm comfortable with those traditional terms. That's not to say those terms are ideal and it's not to say they are right for everybody. Some people say God should always be referred to as God, avoiding the pronoun altogether, but I find that rather awkward and forced. Since we're accustomed to using pronouns, it sounds odd when we don't. On a rather silly note, would "they" be an acceptable pronoun since God is triune?

 Beyond language is the understanding that God is God. Beyond description. Beyond imagination. Certainly beyond human structures and categories. Ineffable. God.

God's Word is beyond language. The Bible we have on paper (and on apps) describes, within the culture of the time, the authority and relational nature of our infinite God by using finite words. Beyond nouns, pronouns, and adjectives is the reality that God is God. Beyond description. Beyond imagination. Certainly beyond human structures and categories. Ineffable. God.

We are made in the image of the infinite and indescribable God, not in physical ways, but in ways that are infinitely and indescribably more important. We love. We create. We think and reason.

So to honor God we should do all of those things for the glory of God. Love God. Love your neighbor. Use your imagination. Think creatively to make the world a better place. Praise God from whom all blessings flow with words, song, art. Expand your mind. Broaden your knowledge. Question God. Ask why . . . not in the sense of questioning God's love or wisdom and not to question Gods' sovereignty, but in the sense you want to know the mind of God . . . to come to know the God in whose image we are created.

One more thing: I have a Bible app on my phone. Occasionally I receive a message that it needs updating. What is there to update? It's the Bible (I know, I'm just kidding).

Things to Think About:

✓ How do you picture God? How do you refer to God?

✓ How do you conceive of an infinite God? How do you talk about an ineffable God?

✓ Do you ask questions of God? How do you come to know God?

GOD'S PLAN

With this mind, we constantly pray for you, that our God may count you worthy of his calling, and that by his power he may bring to fruition your every desire for goodness and your every deed prompted by faith. We pray this so that the name of our Lord Jesus may be glorified in you, and you in him, according to the grace of our God and the Lord Jesus Christ.

II THESSALONIANS 1:11-12.

God gives us just enough to seek him, and never enough to fully find him. To do more would inhibit our freedom, and our freedom is very dear to God.

MOTHER SAINT RAPHAEL IN MYSTERY AND DESIRE BY RON HANSEN

saw a Facebook post not long ago that has been on my mind and I can't seem to shake it. A young woman I know posted a "praise" because her boyfriend had been called up from AAA baseball to the big league club. She believes it is God's "perfect plan" that he be a major league pitcher. I think that's way off base! How's that for a pun?

Now I am very happy he made it to the majors. That's wonderful. But what bothers me is how we can be quick to praise God when things are going the way we want yet not quite so quick when God does not meet our approval. Will she post a praise of God's "perfect plan" if he's sent back to the minors or if he blows out his arm? I certainly hope those things don't happen, but if they do, that must have been God's plan as well. So she should be just as quick to update her

Facebook page then. After all, the Bible says we should be thankful in all circumstances (I Thessalonians 5:18) . . . good times and bad.

It seems to me that if you think God is directly responsible for the joys, then he is also directly responsible for the sorrows, and I have a problem with that. I don't believe God has a specific plan for our lives in the sense that God moves us around like pieces on a chess board.

For example, I just don't see God having an intentional plan for us to marry a specific person . . . not if we have freedom of choice.

Let's say I decide to get married at a time in life when I am out of tune with God's "perfect plan." I'm more concerned with what I want and when I want it than I am with what God desires. I'm more concerned with myself than I am with God and other people. So in this time of selfishness I marry the wrong person . . . which means she has married the wrong person, too. Because of that choice, two people are married to the wrong person . . . each other. And what about the people they should have married? Now they'll be married to the wrong people. It never ends.

Either we are free to marry the one we choose (and who chooses us) or God "perfectly plans" who we marry and we have no choice. Considering all the bad marriages in our country today, something is out of whack. And it's not God . . . it's us.

It's probably a good idea for me to say here that I am very glad I chose my lovely wife, Carole, and I am very glad (and thankful) she chose me. Could I have been just as happy with another special someone? Possibly. But I also know that being married to Carole is as good as it gets. We choose each other every day.

I have no doubt God loves us and cares for us. I have no doubt God is active and present in our lives. But God loving us and wanting what is good for us does not mean God controls us. True love, true relationship requires freedom; otherwise it's not relationship at all, it's possession. God desires love and relationship, so God in his infinite love has given us the freedom to choose . . . to say yes . . . or no.

It's not God's intentional will we marry a particular person, live in a designated town, or hold a specific job (like major league pitcher) . . . as good as marriage, home, and career may be. And it's certainly not God's intentional will bad things happen to us. We do, however, live within the circumstances of a practical world. The rules apply to all of us. The rules of physics, the rules of nature, the rules of human relationships apply to everyone. If we make good choices, good things are likely to follow. If we make bad choices, bad things are likely to follow. And it's important to understand we don't live in a vacuum . . . we live in community. The choices we make impact not only ourselves but untold people around us. And their choices impact us.

✓ I have no doubt God loves us and cares for us. I have no doubt God is active and present in our lives. But God loving us and wanting what is good for us does not mean God controls us. True love, true relationship requires freedom; otherwise it's not relationship at all, it's possession.

Here's how I see it within the limits of my fuzzy, myopic theological vision: The perfect plan of God within this imperfect world is that we love the Lord our God with all our heart, soul, mind, and strength and that we love our neighbor as ourselves. If we love God and love our families, friends, classmates, co-workers, and everyone else who fits into the grand "who is my neighbor?" category as we should, the other things will fall into place.

Whenever we ponder this idea of "God's plan" we have to remind ourselves we have a limited point of view . . . in both space and time. God is bigger than his creation (infinitely bigger) and sees the complete picture when we can't. God is beyond time where we have to live within linear time. God knows what was, is, and shall be when all we have is now. We don't even have a true grasp of the past because our memories and perceptions are so limited.

So where does that put us in this practical world? We all have unique gifts and talents, so we should do the best we can with what we've got for God and each other. For example, when making decisions (even small ones), we should ask ourselves how it fits into the bigger picture. How does it love, honor, and respect God and how does it love, honor, and respect other people? And, also very important, how does it love, honor, and respect ourselves? It's about love and grace being at the center of who we are and what we do.

You're at a place in life when you'll be making many tough decisions. You will be living on your own, developing a career, getting married, raising a family. God has given you the wonderful gift of intelligence, so think. God is present in this world, so pray without ceasing. Love God. Love your neighbor. Do the right things for the right reasons. God will honor that and good things will happen . . . for you and for others, too.

There will be plenty of twists and turns along the way. Occasionally, you'll come to a fork in the road. You have the freedom to choose. Choose love.

One more thing: Leslie Weatherhead's *The Will of God*[16] does a wonderful job of explaining the idea of God's intentional, circumstantial and ultimate will. I highly recommend it.

Things to Think About:

✓ What does the idea of God's "perfect plan" mean to you?

✓ What's the difference between making something happen (intentional will) and allowing something to happen (circumstantial will)?

✓ How are you in relationship with God?

✓ If someone said to you, "John died in that car crash because God wanted him in heaven," how would you respond?

JOY

May the God of hope fill you with all joy and peace
as you trust in him, so that you may overflow with hope
by the power of the Holy Spirit.
ROMANS 15:13

Joy is the infallible sign of the presence of God.
PIERRE TEILHARD DE CHARDIN

I remember being at a church youth gathering once where a young woman, probably about sixteen or seventeen years old, asked to play the piano. She wanted to perform and, to her credit, it was quite apparent that her goal was to perform to the glory of God, not to bring attention to herself. There was one small problem though. She couldn't play, not very well at least. She was struggling. She was painfully struggling . . . to the point it became clear she just didn't have any musical talent. Then she paused and announced she felt called by God to play the piano and to play that night for the group. And she continued on until it mercifully (for her and us) came to an end.

I must admit I admired her courage. Performing in front of one's peers (or any audience for that matter) is difficult in the best of circumstances. It must have been terrifying for her. She had to know she wasn't much of a player. Maybe she was expecting a miracle.

I have always wondered why she thought she was called to play the piano. Where did that come from? From herself? From her parents?

Maybe it did come from God. It's certainly not for me to say. And miracles are always possible when God is involved.

However, it was obvious she didn't have the talent for it. And based on that performance and other comments she made as the evening went along, she was just not cut out for the piano. In fact, she went on to admit she was pretty miserable trying and found no joy in playing.

 It seems to me if we are called to do something we will find joy in it, and I think that sense of joy is a good sign we're on the right track.

Now that's not to say we shouldn't stretch ourselves and try new things. Of course we should. We never know what we can do until we try, until we commit ourselves to study and practice. We never know how God might be molding us as God completes us. But I'm really not talking about effort here. And I don't intend this to be about misery . . . it's joy, actually.

I just don't believe it is God's intent to make us miserable. That's not to say our work won't be challenging. Of course it will be. In fact, most everything worthwhile requires hard work and dedication. It may be stressful, frustrating, frightening. It may even be dangerous. But it seems to me if we are truly called to do something we will find joy in it, and I think that sense of joy is a good sign we're on the right track. There should be a feeling of peace and satisfaction that comes from the work. Maybe that's God trying to tell us something. And if that sense of joy isn't there, maybe that's God trying to tell us something, too.

Things to Think About:

✓ What work brings you the most joy? What are your talents and skills?

✓ Do you think God would call you to work that makes you miserable or at which you are doomed to fail?

✓ What's the hardest thing you've ever done that also brought you the most joy? Why?

LOOKING FOR GOD

Suppose one of you has a hundred sheep and loses one of them.
Doesn't he leave the ninety-nine in the open country and
go after the lost sheep until he finds it? And when he finds it,
he joyfully puts it on his shoulders and goes home.
Then he calls his friends and neighbors together and says,
'Rejoice with me; I have found my lost sheep.'
LUKE 15:4-6

If you have found God with great ease,
perhaps it is not God you have found.
THOMAS MERTON

When I was a little fellow, about three or four years old, our family went to Panama City, Florida on a family vacation. One afternoon we were shopping in one of those touristy souvenir stores. You know the kind—with the shells and postcards and t-shirts. I probably needed something really important like a bucket or a straw hat. Anyway, we were in the store and when my mom turned her head for a second I wandered off. I don't recall how I managed to do this, but somehow I got lost. Let me point out here it's not that my mom wasn't paying attention. Of course she was . . . she always did. It's just that little kids are really quick and can get away before you know it.

Once I realized Mom was gone (at least that's what I thought), I started looking for her and when I didn't see her in the store, I walked outside to look. I ended up crossing a street and going into a grocery

173

store. Now, I know that doesn't make sense, but I was just a little kid and little kids do crazy things when they get scared. As you can imagine, everyone was frantically searching the souvenir store. Thinking back on it, I'm glad my parents did come looking for me rather than running off . . . that could have been their chance for freedom . . . but I digress.

✓ Mom has always said I was sitting on the check-out counter crying my head off. I wanted to find her, but I didn't know how. And the more I panicked, the more lost I became. I just had to stop so she could find me.

Their search had gotten to the point where they realized I wasn't in the souvenir store, so they spread out from there. As they were checking any place they could imagine, Mom finally came rushing into the grocery store, and there I was being taken care of by a nice lady who worked there. Mom has always said I was sitting on the check-out counter crying my little head off. I wanted to find her, but I didn't know how. And the more I panicked, the more lost I became. I just had to stop so she could find me.

I often think that to God it must seem like we're all a bunch of lost kids. We get distracted. We wander away. We panic and run off to the wrong places. I wandered off from my mom. She didn't turn away from me. She came looking for me. And God will never turn away either. He won't give up on us. He won't hide from us and he certainly won't run off and leave us behind. He keeps reaching out to us.

We may be lost and confused, but he'll find us. We may be sitting on the check-out counter crying our little heads off, but he'll find us. All we have to do is open our hearts and reach out to him as he comes to take us home.

Things to Think About:

✓ Have you ever been lost? How did it feel when you realized you didn't know where you were? How did you find your way back?

✓ There were quite a few people looking for me when I got lost. How can you help someone who may not know their way home?

✓ Is it up to us to look for God or does God find us where we are? What's the difference?

✓ How do we open our hearts and reach out to God?

THE VOICE OF GOD

The LORD said, 'Go out and stand on the mountain in the presence of the LORD, for the LORD is about to pass by.' Then a great and powerful wind tore the mountains apart and shattered the rocks before the LORD, but the LORD was not in the wind. After the wind there was an earthquake, but the LORD was not in the earthquake. After the earthquake came a fire, but the LORD was not in the fire. And after the fire came a gentle whisper.

I KINGS 19:11-12

Earth's crammed with heaven, And every common bush afire with God; But only he who sees, takes off his shoes— The rest sit round it and pluck blackberries.

ELIZABETH BARRETT BROWNING

God can speak in a loud booming voice. Or God can get our attention in other ways, too. You know, burning bushes, choirs of angels, and that sort of thing. But that's pretty rare. Most of the time God speaks in a gentle whisper. A still, small voice.

I must admit there are times in my life when I would prefer that God just shout out what I want to know. An audible answer to an audible question would be nice . . . and easy. Maybe God could respond like a Magic 8 Ball.™ Now, that would be convenient.

Perhaps the real problem with hearing the voice of God is not that God is silent, but that I'm not listening and not paying attention to how and when God does speak. It is for us to go to the mountain to stand in the presence of the Lord as he passes by. It's for us to notice the world that is aflame with God's presence.

That may not be literally true. We don't necessarily have to climb a mountain, although the mountains can be a very spiritual place. We don't have to scan the sky looking for smoke from the burning bush, but I do think we have to look up from the beaten path and see the fire of a sunset. We have to put away the distractions and switch off the noise.

 Perhaps the real problem with hearing the voice of God is not that God is silent, but that I'm not listening and not paying attention to how and when God does speak.

Different people have their own ways of listening for God. And God has his own way of speaking to different people. For me, it's going out alone in the woods or on the river. In nature I am reminded of the majesty of God, and I find the quiet time that comes with hiking and fly fishing to be very revealing. God and I visit together in those places.

God speaks in his own voice in his own time (no matter how inconvenient we think that may be). We must stop and listen. Consider and ponder. Wait upon the Lord who will surely come.

Things to Think About:

✓ How do you listen for God's still, small voice?

✓ How do you deal with noise and distractions in your life?

✓ Do you have a special place where you feel closest to God? Have you considered creating such a place? What would it be?

✓ Have you ever considered that God may speak through you to other people?

PRAY WITHOUT CEASING

Rejoice always; pray continually; give thanks in all circumstances;
for this is God's will for you in Christ Jesus.
I THESSALONIANS 5:16-18

Do not think of solitude as being alone, but as being alone
with God. Do not think of silence as not speaking,
but as listening to God. Do not think of prayer as
talking to God, but as resting in God.
HENRI NOUWEN

The Bible says we should pray continually, or as the King James Version has it, "pray without ceasing." That sounds a little odd. I always get this mental picture of some guy walking around with his head bowed and eyes closed, bumping into light poles and tripping over curbs.

I think it's all about how you define prayer. There is the traditional way of praying where we bow our heads and close our eyes. Then there is praying that has to do with how we live our lives. Some people refer to it as prayerful living. To me, to pray without ceasing means I live my life as if Jesus were with me all of the time. We are constant companions involved in a never-ending conversation.

I have to admit, though, I often do things that disrupt the conversation (I think that's what sin is—fracturing our communion with God). But my goal is to go through life with the attitude that I want Jesus with me all the time . . . not in the physical sense, of course, but in a spiritual communion kind of way. I want him to be a part of what I do, who I spend time with, what I talk about. Like I said, I don't always get it right, but I'm trying.

 My goal is to go through life with the attitude that I want Jesus with me all the time. I want him to be a part of what I do, who I spend time with, what I talk about.

I've found continuing prayer to be helpful with moral and ethical questions, too. You've heard the saying "What would Jesus do?" Well, it seems to me, if I'm praying without ceasing, my answer to that question would be, "He's standing right here. I'll ask him."

One more thing: In your continuing prayer, I would encourage you to be honest with God. You might as well be honest, it's not like you can hide from God. If there is something on your mind, tell God about it. If you're mad, confused, doubting, then say it. God can handle whatever you bring. He's not going to be embarrassed. You're not going to hurt his feelings. You certainly can't insult God in any way that hasn't already been done. Besides, there's nothing we can do to diminish or enhance God in any way. God is God no matter what. So tell God what's on your mind. I truly believe God appreciates honesty. He gets too much of the other stuff as it is.

Things to Think About:

✓ What does "pray continually" mean to you?

✓ What does it mean to you to live in a "spiritual communion" kind of way?

✓ Do you find it difficult being honest with God?

TEAM JESUS

When Jesus entered the temple courts, he began to drive out those who were selling. 'It is written,' he said to them, 'My house will be a house of prayer; but you have made it a den of robbers.'
LUKE 19:45-46

The more one respects Jesus, the more one must be brokenhearted, embarrassed, furious, or some combination thereof when one considers what we Christians have done with Jesus. That's certainly true when it comes to calling Jesus Lord, something we Christians do a lot, often without the foggiest idea of what we mean. Has he become (I shudder to ask this) less our Lord and more our Mascot?
BRIAN D. MCLAREN

I was in a Christian bookstore the other day and was amazed at all of the stuff that was in there. I don't mean books (they had lots of those, of course). I'm talking about all of the other stuff: key chains, posters, games, jewelry, t-shirts, bumper stickers. It was everywhere—from floor to ceiling. They say Jesus Saves, but it looks like Jesus Sells, too.

It's not all bad. A simple cross necklace could be nice. And I always thought the W.W.J.D. bracelets served as a good reminder of who we are as Christians. But some of this stuff has gotten way out of hand . . .

Jesus fish belt buckle (uphold your faith and your pants).

Jesus fishing lures (for fishers of men and fishers of bass).

The Birth of Jesus Pop Up (pop out?) Book.

Jesus bobble head doll (Wouldn't a John the Baptist bobble head be more appropriate?).

I once saw a guy wearing a t-shirt with a picture of Jesus on the front (I've always wondered how they knew what Jesus looked like, but that's another issue). What happens when that shirt gets old and worn out? It seems wrong to throw it into the rag bag. I just can't imagine dusting my Apostles Action Figures or wiping up spilled sacramental wine with Jesus—even if that's not what he really looked like. Should the shirt be given an honorary burial? And if you bury a Jesus shirt will it rise up out of the ground after three days?

 Jesus is not a merchandising opportunity, and he's not a favorite team we support by wearing shirts and yelling cheers and putting bumper stickers on our cars.

I know I'm being silly and maybe a little sacrilegious. I realize a lot of "religious merchandise" is marketed by people who have absolutely no concern for our faith. They are just looking to make a buck. However, I also think Christians produce and purchase so much silly and sacrilegious junk that we can no longer tell the difference. Jesus is not a merchandising opportunity, and he's not a favorite team we support by wearing shirts and yelling cheers and putting bumper stickers on our cars. Considering his angry response to the money changers at the temple, how do you think he feels about this? Do you really think this is what Jesus would do?

Some people may say they wear these things as a witness, but it seems to me that trivializing the majesty of God is not a positive witness. And besides, witnessing is not what you wear, it's how you live your life. I've always wondered if my car broke down and I found myself stranded on the side of the road, how many cars with fish emblems on the back would go rocketing by. As Christians, we must pull over on the highway of life and love our neighbor. That's the best witness of all. That's what Jesus did.

Things to Think About:

✓ If Jesus is fashionable, does that mean he will go out of style?

✓ Where do you draw the line between reasonable and offensive . . . enduring and trendy?

✓ What is the difference between Jesus as Lord and Jesus as Mascot?

✓ What's the most kitschy religious item you've ever seen?

SIN

Be perfect, therefore, as your heavenly Father is perfect.
MATTHEW 5:48

Child, God is not angry with you. Come home and don't be afraid.
CAROLE SMITH

When I was a kid in Sunday School, I was taught not to sin and was given a list of things I shouldn't do . . . things like don't lie, don't cheat, don't steal. And some of the items on the list were positive, too. I was also taught things I should be sure to do. I should love God, love my neighbor, honor my parents. But I have to admit, the "shalt nots" usually got much more attention than the "shalts."

A list can be a good thing. It can be a starting point to teach us things we need to know—especially as children. We do need to learn to not lie, cheat, and steal. And we do need to learn to love God, love our neighbor, and honor our parents. Those are very important lessons we should all remember . . . children and adults. Just think how much better the world would be if there was no lying, cheating, and stealing and if everyone loved God, loved their neighbor, and honored their parents. We wouldn't recognize the place.

I have to say, I've always been amazed at the common sense of the Bible. It's not just a collection of rules for the sake of rules. There is a remarkable amount of practical reality there.

For example, in Exodus 20:5 (and a couple of other places, too) the Bible says the sins of the fathers will be visited upon the heads of the children and grandchildren. I'll admit that can be a difficult passage to deal with. After all, why should innocent children be punished for something they had no control over? I think it's just recognizing practical reality. Look around at the children in your community. A child's performance in school is directly linked to parental involvement . . . or the lack of it. Obese parents typically have obese children. People from divorced families are more likely to be divorced themselves. Abused children often grow into abusive adults. Exodus chapter twenty is simply an acknowledgement of the reality of the world. We don't live in the world as separate individuals. Rather, we live in the world as a community of individuals. So our actions, be they good or bad, impact each other for generations.

And that brings us back to the idea of the list. Like I said, a list can be a good thing . . . especially when we're just starting out. But the problem with any list—no matter how practical it may be—is that it often turns into a rule book or checklist. Then life becomes all about following the rules and checking things off the list. Life becomes law rather than grace. Life becomes rule rather than relationship. I think that's why Jesus had such a problem with the Pharisees. They knew all about the rules, but they knew nothing about living in relationship with God or with their neighbor.

Let me pause here to say the Pharisees were not villains. We should never make them be the bad guys in black hats. They were devoted religious leaders who dedicated their lives to understanding how God would have them live. The problem was they got lost in the regulations and customs of the day. I have to admit, I worry about being a Pharisee myself. It's so easy to fall into the trap of living life by a checklist, then judging and condemning people who don't follow my rulebook. It's so easy to make a list of the standards I favor while omitting the ones I explain away or just ignore. Yes, lists can be good and rules can be good, but not in and of themselves. They direct us to something much bigger. They direct us to communion and to community.

For that reason, I understand sin to be anything that separates us from God and breaks our relationship with God, with God's children, and with all of God's creation. Now, we may say there are things we do (acts of commission) and things we don't do (acts of omission) that cause the separation, and there is certainly a connection. However, the problem with that approach is it takes us back to lists and rules . . . rules that say you must not do some things, you must do others.

✓ It seems to me sin is not so much what we do or don't do . . . those things are merely symptoms. Sin is not the act that breaks the relationship. Sin, rather, is the breaking of the relationship that leads to the act. Sin is when I turn from God and into myself.

It seems to me sin is not so much what we do or don't do . . . those things are merely symptoms. Sin is not the act that breaks the relationship. Sin, rather, is the breaking of the relationship that leads to the act. Sin is when I turn from God and into myself. It's when the love of self, the love of I, overtakes the love of God and the love of other people. That's when bad things start to happen and it's those bad things that are the evidence of the broken relationship.

When my wonderful son, Harry, was a little kid, my lovely wife, Carole, and I would teach him the do's and don'ts of life because we loved him and wanted what was best for him. At that age, it was really all he was ready for . . . eat your vegetables . . . brush your teeth . . . don't run into the street. It was much more about the rule than the reason. And by the way, don't ever debate a two year old . . . you'll never win. "Because I said so" is a perfectly good answer . . . for a time.

As he matured into an adult, our relationship matured because we love him and want what is best for him. Harry began to understand the reason of those earlier lists and rules as the old "because I said so" developed into rational and respectful discussion. In his maturity, he began to make decisions, not based on rules, but based on relationship with us . . . grounded in knowledge, understanding, and reason.

In a sense, it's the same in our relationship with God. When we are young in the faith, helpful lists, rules, and guides can be good things, but they are always limited and limiting. As we mature, we can begin to seek the knowledge, understanding, and reason of God. We come to know the mind of God as God is revealed to us. We come to know that God loves us and wants what's best for us.

I want to know the ones I love the most. I want to spend time with the ones I love the most. I want to give myself to the ones I love the most with all of my heart and soul and mind and strength. That is the foundation for relationship, communion, and community.

God is love and love is at the foundation of all God does with us and for us. Love should be the foundation of all we do with and for each other. Sin is broken love, a broken foundation, that leads to very bad things which are visited upon our heads for many generations.

And then there is grace . . .

Things to Think About:

✓ Are there "to do" and "to don't" lists you find helpful? Harmful?

✓ How do you see the "sins of the fathers" impacting other generations?

✓ Do you agree there are some sins we pay special attention to while others we ignore?

✓ What does it mean to "know" the ones we love the most? To "know" God?

GRACE

For as high as the heavens are above the earth, so great is his
love for those who fear him; as far as the east is from the west,
so far has he removed our transgressions from us.
PSALM 103:11-12

Through many dangers, toils and snares
I have already come;
'Tis grace that brought me safe thus far,
And grace shall lead me home.
JOHN NEWTON (AMAZING GRACE)

People much smarter than I am have written libraries of books explaining the theology of grace. I'm not even going to try. What I do want to try is this: Grace is a gift. Take it. Say, "Yes, please. Thank you."

Grace is God's gift of love for us that is undeserved, unmerited, unfair, and absolutely wonderful.[17] Too good to be true, yet it is. It is God saying to us, "I love you. I forgive you. All is well. Today is a brand new day." Grace is God wrapping his arms around us.

Grace may indeed sound too good to be true, but I have no trouble believing it is. I can accept the idea that God forgives me. God is love after all, so grace naturally follows.

The hard part of grace for me is actually forgiving myself. How egotistical could I possibly be? God forgives me but I cannot? If the holy and righteous God, creator and sustainer of all things, is willing—even eager—to forgive me, how can I have the audacity to not forgive myself? Who am I to say to God, "Well, you can forgive and forget if you want to, but I'm holding on to my past no matter what?"

 Grace is God wrapping his arms around us.

God is God. I am not . . . we are not. God forgives. So should I . . . so should we all. Amazing grace. Yes, please. Thank you.

Things to Think About:

✓ How do you describe grace?

✓ How do you know God's grace in your life?

✓ Are there grace-filled people you know? How might you offer grace to someone?

✓ Why is it hard for us to forgive ourselves? Why do we keep reliving the past?

GOD IS NOT AN ERRAND BOY

Suppose a brother or sister is without clothes and daily food.
If one of you says to them, 'Go in peace; keep warm and well fed,'
but does nothing about their physical needs, what good is it? In the
same way, faith by itself, if not accompanied by action, is dead.

JAMES 2:15-17

One of the most insidious maladies of our time [is]: the tendency
in most of us to observe rather than act, avoid rather than
participate, not do rather than do; the tendency to give in to the
sly, negative, cautionary voices that constantly counsel us to be
careful, to be controlled, to be wary and prudent and hesitant and
guarded in our approach of this complicated thing called living.

ARTHUR GORDON

I have to admit I sometimes get the feeling my prayers are more about talking than listening, more about what I want than what others need, and more about giving directions than looking for guidance. Now, I do believe God wants us to pray and that involves talking as well as listening. I also believe God wants us to pray for things we need even though that means our attention is on ourselves. In fact, John 16:24 says that if we ask we will receive so that our joy may be full. We should take all of our worries, concerns, and requests to God in prayer. That's a good thing. And we should pray for other people. That's a good thing, too. James 5:16 says that we should pray for each other and that the prayer of a righteous person has great power. Praying for ourselves is good. Praying for others is good.

Having said that, however, I think there's more to it. I think there's a problem when we're quick to point things out and slow to follow through ourselves. That's what I mean by giving directions rather than seeking guidance. Maybe it's easy to forget that God is not the great Santa Claus in the sky filling orders we mail in each night with our bedtime prayers.

 Maybe it's easy to forget that God is not the great Santa Claus in the sky filling orders we mail in each night with our bedtime prayers.

In his song, "When You Gonna Wake Up," Bob Dylan asks, "Do you ever wonder just what God requires? You think He's just an errand boy to satisfy your wandering desires."[18] It seems to me rather than just telling God what needs to be done, we should look for ways to do it ourselves. We should never just sit back and expect God to take care of things for us.

Yes, I believe we should pray for other people. We should ask for healing or comfort or peace or whatever is appropriate. And no, it's not that God needs to be pointed in the right direction. He knows before we ask. It's through prayer that God allows us to participate in his work.

And, of course, we should ask God for guidance and strength. We'd be lost without it. The fact of the matter is some things (most things really) we cannot do on our own. There are mysteries of God we aren't capable of understanding—especially when it comes to how God works in other people's lives. But there comes a point when we should go out in prayerful communion with God using the abilities and talents with which we have been blessed.

God has given us brains with which to think and reason. We are creative. We have the great honor of participating in God's grace, so we must look for ways we can do our part. For example, praying for a friend who is hurting is a good thing. Praying for a friend who is hurting then going to spend time with that person is better. And let's face it, that's harder to do. It takes time, effort, commitment, and emotional investment . . . even vulnerability.

The point is this: We should open ourselves for God to work through us as we look for ways to do what needs to be done. Anything we ask God to do, we must be willing to work toward ourselves whenever possible . . . and sometimes even when it seems impossible.

Things to Think About:

✓ What does it mean to pray for someone? Can prayer also be physical action and involvement?

✓ How does God allow us to participate in his work? How have you participated in God's work? What was the result?

✓ Who do you know who needs your prayers . . . and your presence?

✓ What are your skills and talents? How are they being used?

DO SOMETHING

For this reason, since the day we heard about you, we have not stopped praying for you. We continually ask God to fill you with the knowledge of his will through all the wisdom and understanding that the Spirit gives, so that you may live a life worthy of the Lord and please him in every way: bearing fruit in every good work, growing in the knowledge of God, being strengthened with all power according to his glorious might so that you may have great endurance and patience, and giving joyful thanks to the Father, who has qualified you to share in the inheritance of his holy people in the kingdom of light.

COLOSSIANS 1:9-12.

When focusing on talents, we tend to forget that our real gift is not so much what we can do, but who we are. The real question is not, 'What can we offer each other,' but 'Who can we be for each other?' No doubt, it is wonderful when we can repair something for a neighbor, give helpful advice to a friend, offer wise counsel to a colleague, bring healing to a patient, or announce good news to a parishioner, but there is a greater gift than all of this. It is the gift of our own life that shines through all we do.

HENRI NOUWEN

There is an old story I really like. It's probably been told a million times (and that may not be an exaggeration), but it's a good one: A gray-haired lady was walking along the beach after a storm. On the beach were hundreds of starfish that had washed up on the shore. As she walked along, she would reach down, pick up a starfish and toss it back into the water. A young man fishing in the surf saw her and asked, "What are you doing?" "Well," the woman said, "I'm just throwing these starfish back in the water as I walk along the beach." The man said, "Why bother? There are hundreds of starfish on the beach and you can't possibly make a difference." The gray-haired lady looked down, picked up a starfish, and tossed it into the water. She smiled and said, "I made a difference to that one."[19]

I have always believed most people want to do good things. They want to help. They want to contribute. They want to make the world a little better place.

The problem we all run into is where to start and what to do. We want to do good work and make a difference in some way, but we don't know how. And the odd thing is, since we don't know exactly what to do we can fall into the trap of not doing anything. Because of our frustration in searching for the perfect contribution, we make no contribution at all.

I think the answer to this problem is to just do something (insert your own shoe commercial reference here). Just do anything, no matter how small or insignificant it may seem. Then one good turn will lead to another. There will always be plenty to do right where we are.

Sometimes we fall into the trap of thinking real missions work takes place away from home, but I think that's a mistake. And let me be quick to add here that mission trips are a very good thing. Jesus did say "Go into all the world" after all. The Great Commission is not a suggestion. As United Methodist Bishop Sally Dyck once said, "What part of 'go' do you not understand?"[20]

However (I know you could see that coming a mile away), we have to be careful that mission trips do not become religious tourism. For example, I wonder how many times a missions team from Alabama loads up a van to travel to work in West Virginia and along the way passes a missions team from West Virginia traveling to work in Alabama? I wonder how many millions of dollars have been spent on airline tickets and hotel rooms in "mission fields" around the country and around the world?

✓ What if we took some of the money we spend on planes, trains, and automobiles and used it for hurting people in our own hometowns? Better yet, what if we took some of the time and energy involved in fund-raising and travel and spent it *with* hurting people in our own hometowns . . . getting to know them and building relationships with them?

What if we took some of the money we spend on planes, trains, and automobiles and used it for hurting people in our own hometowns? Better yet, what if we took some of the time and energy involved in fund-raising and travel and spent it *with* hurting people in our own hometowns . . . getting to know them and building relationships with them? Of course, that's not nearly as adventuresome. Home is boring. Other places and other people are exciting. And perhaps it's easier that way, too, because there is less commitment. When the short-term trip is over we go back to our regular lives with our regular friends, but with hometown missions those pesky people are with us all the time . . . and hurting all the time. The point is this: Missions should always be about love, relationship, and service—at home, across the country, or around the world. Missions should never be about exotic destinations, group bonding, and cool photos.

Many people will have the opportunity to work in some far-away land. It is often a life-changing experience for everyone involved. We all have the opportunity to work at home—to bloom where we're planted. It, too, is often a life-changing experience for everyone involved.

All we have to do is look around for what needs doing and who needs loving. Look around at school. Look around at work. Look out the front door. For that matter, just turn around and look inside at the people we live with. There are starfish all over the place.

Things to Think About:

✓ Do you think most people want to help in some way or are they more concerned about their own problems?

✓ What's a small thing you've done that turned out to be more important than you expected?

✓ How has a small thing led to more and maybe bigger things?

✓ What's the difference between missions of love, relationship, and service and religious tourism?

✓ Can you think of a "starfish" who could use a little help?

BLESSINGS

Therefore if you have any encouragement from being united with
Christ, if any comfort from his love, if any common sharing in
the Spirit, if any tenderness and compassion, then make my joy
complete by being like-minded, having the same love, being one in
spirit and of one mind. Do nothing out of selfish ambition or vain
conceit. Rather, in humility value others above yourselves, not looking
to your own interests but each of you to the interests of the others.
PHILIPPIANS 2:1-4

The single greatest cause of atheism in the world today is
Christians who acknowledge Jesus with their lips, then walk
out the door and deny Him by their lifestyle. That is what an
unbelieving world simply finds unbelievable.
BRENNAN MANNING

When we think about God blessing us it is usually in the sense of what God is going to do for us. God gave me something or God did something for me. That's not necessarily a bad thing, but it can be rather self-centered.

The greatness of Jesus came not through what God did for Jesus. The greatness of Jesus came in what God did through Jesus; how God blessed the world through Jesus and how Jesus responded to the call of God—a response that took him to the cross and out of the tomb.

Likewise, our blessing comes not in what God does for us (since it's not about us) but in what God does through us (because it is

203

about other people). Our blessing comes as God blesses others through us.

 Our blessing comes not in what God does for us (since it's not about us) but in what God does through us.

As we seek the blessing of God in this way, our "belief" moves from mere assent (acknowledging particular statements of faith) to action (living a life of love for God and neighbor).

Things to Think About:

✓ Do you agree or disagree that the desire for God's blessings in our lives can be self-centered?

✓ How are we blessed as God blesses others through us?

✓ How has God touched others through your actions?

SMALL KINDNESSES

Therefore, as God's chosen people, holy and dearly loved,
clothe yourselves with compassion, kindness,
humility, gentleness and patience.
COLOSSIANS 3:12

Being considerate of others will take your children
further in life than any college degree.
MARIAN WRIGHT ANDERSON

Everybody has a bad day on occasion. And then there are those people who always have bad days. It's like they plan on it. They are convinced from the moment they get out of bed in the morning they're headed for a bad day. They're right . . . and they'll drag down as many people with them as they possibly can.

Life is tough at times. School is hard. Work is hard. Bad things happen. People can be mean and hateful. That is the reality of the world.

The key is to not wallow in it. Look for good things. Oftentimes, the best thing to do when you're feeling bad is to go do something nice for somebody else. I have to admit though, on a certain level that sounds a little strange. It's the idea that you can make yourself feel better by helping somebody who is worse off than you. And there is always somebody worse off than you. They hurt more so you should feel lucky. Weird, ain't it? Well, that's not really what it's about.

It's about kindness and reaching out to others. It could be the person we help is facing a bad situation. In fact, we really never know what someone else is going through. And we certainly never know what goes on behind closed doors.

The point is to make an effort to do good whenever and wherever we can . . . big or small. When we share the love of God we are comforted by the love of God.

Some people are convinced from the moment they get out of bed in the morning they're headed for a bad day. Those people are right . . . and they'll drag down as many people with them as they possibly can.

The people we help usually return that love (but not always, and that's okay, too). We go to help them and they end up helping us more than we could ever imagine. Weird, ain't it? And very cool.

Things to Think About:

✓ Why are some people determined to be miserable? How can you be determined to help them have a better day?

✓ How does helping someone else make you feel better?

✓ What's a small thing someone has done for you? What was the size of the impact relative to the size of the kindness?

HOLIDAY TREE

And there were shepherds living out in the fields nearby, keeping watch over their flocks at night. An angel of the Lord appeared to them, and the glory of the Lord shone around them, and they were terrified. But the angel said to them, 'Do not be afraid. I bring you good news that will cause great joy for all the people. Today in the town of David a Savior has been born to you; he is the Messiah, the Lord.'

LUKE 2:8-11

It might be easy to run away to a monastery, away from the commercialization, the hectic hustle, the demanding family responsibilities of Christmas-time. Then we would have a holy Christmas. But we would forget the lesson of the Incarnation, of the enfleshing of God . . . the lesson that we who are followers of Jesus do not run from the secular; rather we try to transform it. It is our mission to make holy the secular aspects of Christmas just as the early Christians baptized the Christmas tree. And we do this by being holy people . . . kind, patient, generous, loving, laughing people . . . no matter how maddening is the Christmas rush.

FR. ANDREW GREELEY

'm writing these thoughts the Friday after Thanksgiving . . . the high holy day of shopping. People have been up before the sun fighting over sweaters, coffee makers, and televisions. The fight has also begun over the annual Christmas vs. Holidays controversy. What should people say . . . Merry Christmas or Happy Holidays? When we light the big green plant on the town square, what should we call it . . . Christmas Tree or Holiday Tree?

I think the whole tree thing is just silly. Regardless of whatever inclusive name is used now, it's been a Christmas tree for 500 years. Inclusiveness is fine, but if we're going to celebrate diversity shouldn't Christmas be included in the celebration? And why is it the PC crowd singles out the Christmas tree? I've never heard anyone refer to a Menorah as a Holiday Candelabrum. No one calls Ramadan a Holiday Fast. To do so would be offensive.

✓ There are people who have, in the name of Christ, invested a lot of time, effort, and money in what is essentially a political battle, a noisy skirmish, more volume than substance. The true battle should be the fight against injustice, poverty, pain, loneliness, sickness, and hunger.

There's something deeper going on here. This argument is more about power than the Christmas/Holiday season itself. That is true from both sides. So since I'm a Christian and Jesus teaches me to deal with the beam in my eye rather than the mote in my neighbor's eye, I'll focus on the Christian side of this problem.

There are people who have, in the name of Christ, invested a lot of time, effort, and money in what is essentially a political battle, a noisy skirmish, more volume than substance. The true battle should be the fight against injustice, poverty, pain, loneliness, sickness, and hunger. But I wonder how often these enemies are ignored because we're too busy playing cultural politics. There is too much important work to be done to allow ourselves to be caught up in paltry distractions.

The Salvation Army has the names of disadvantaged children who may not know the joy of opening a gift. The staff of the Food Bank works every day to feed our neighbors who are hungry and malnourished. Local nursing homes and assisted living facilities have residents who are ignored or forgotten. Some of God's children will spend Christmas alone in prison. The list goes on.

As Christians we should remember Jesus didn't fight political battles. His first response was to be intimately involved with the people around him. He fed them, ate with them, listened to them, touched them, loved them.

The spirit of Christmas isn't in decorations, greetings, or retail sales. It isn't up to the shopping mall sales clerks to keep Christ in Christmas by saying Merry Christmas rather than Happy Holidays. They're running a store, not a church. And the reality is there's more than one holiday this time of year and not everyone who shops is Christian. More important, if we're depending on the mall to defend the integrity of Christmas, we've already lost.

If Christ is truly the reason for the season, then it's up to Christians to live as Jesus lived. Loving our neighbors and our enemies. Every day. Merry Christmas.

Things to Think About:

✓ What are your thoughts on Black Friday (and now Cyber Monday) and the culture of shopping that is tied to Christmas?

✓ What do you enjoy most about the Christmas season? Are there things that trouble you?

✓ How do you keep Christ in Christmas? How do you keep Christ throughout the year?

NOTES

1 Ralph Waldo Emerson, *The Essential Writings of Ralph Waldo Emerson* (New York: The Modern Library, 2000), 138.

2 Carl Stephens was one of the best announcers to ever call a game and an even better human being. When Carl announced his retirement, he was referred to as "legendary" in a number of news stories and rightfully so. I'll always be grateful for how kind he was to me during my early days of announcing and how supportive he was years later when I stepped in for him at the microphone.

3 I borrowed this idea from Garrison Keillor and his "News from Lake Woebegone" segment on *A Prairie Home Companion*. On a side note, I once had the privilege of being Mr. Keillor's driver when he was in Opelika for a performance. Our conversation on the short drive from the hotel to the theater was one of the most fascinating conversations I have had in my life. I should have taken a wrong turn to make the drive last longer.

4 J. D. Salinger, *Franny and Zooey* (Boston: Little, Brown & Company, 1961).

5 Rick Warren, *The Purpose Driven Life* (Grand Rapids, MI: Zondervan, 2000), 17.

6 Pat Williams, *Read for Your Life: 11 Ways to Better Yourself Through Books* (Deerfield Beach, FL: Health Communications, Inc, 2007), 61.

7 Alfred, Lord Tennyson, *In Memoriam A.H.H.*

8 Otis Blackwell and Elvis Pressley, *All Shook Up* (RCA, 1957).

9 Gary Chapman, *The Five Love Languages* (Chicago: Northfield Publishing, 1992).

10 For an interesting discussion about how men and women communicate see: John Gray, *Men Are from Mars, Women Are from Venus* (New York: HarperCollins Publishers, 1993).

11 Robert Frost, "The Death of the Hired Man," in *The Road Not Taken* (New York: Henry Holt and Company, 1985), 152-154.

12 Dear Harry, Just because you're grown, don't start thinking I'm not here for you still. I still am and always will be. That will never pass. Memories and letters will remain even when I can't be with you in person. Love, Dad.

13 My thoughts in this letter are greatly influenced by Dr. Godsey's book *When We Talk about God . . . Let's Be Honest* (Macon, GA: Smyth & Hewlys, 1996).

14 Ibid., 21

15 Dietrich Bonhoeffer, *Ethics,* trans. Neville Horton Smith (New York: Touchstone, 1995), 70.

16 Leslie Weatherhead, *The Will of God* (Nashville: Abingdon Press, 1999).

17 Philip Yancey, *What's So Amazing About Grace* (Grand Rapids, MI: Zondervan, 1997), 88.

18 Bob Dylan, *When You Gonna Wake Up* (Special Rider Music, 1979).

19 This story, which has been told in a variety of ways by a variety of people, is adapted from the work of Loren Eiseley, *The Star Thrower* (New York: Mariner Books, 1979).

20 As quoted by Bishop Larry M. Goodpastor (what a cool preacher name) in his Episcopal Address to the Alabama-West Florida Conference of the United Methodist Church, June 6, 2005.

CONNECT WITH THE AUTHOR

Website: everydayisanaudition.com
E-mail: everydayisanaudition@gmail.com
Facebook: facebook.com/everydayisanaudition